"All good TEDx stories are personal ones, very seldomly they're as personal as Jojanneke's at TEDxDelft. Having an idea worth spreading is often not enough, a TEDx speaker needs to be willing to dig to the centre of it to strip it to its core message. Only then will it touch the (online) audience in the heart. When we first met Jojanneke, we knew this was exactly what she was going to do. And she did.

—Rob Speekenbrink, TEDx Senior Ambassador Europe, Founder, Licensee, Curator, Rule Maven @TEDxDelft

"Jojanneke and TEDx: a match made in heaven. A perfect way to learn presentation skills."

—Nico Haasbroek, former editor in chief of Dutch national news broadcasting

"It's just marvelous to be able to see speaking at TEDx from the speaker's point of view. Thanks for letting us be the fly on the wall!"

—Caryn 't Hart de Wijkerslooth, curator TEDxDelft

"An essential book for public speakers. This book explains, metaphorically spoken, what the difference is between playing a jazz improvisation, playing a classical piece and singing a familiar song. Jojanneke shares, from experience and in great detail, what you need to do to be a great speaker and what the difference is between a corporate speech and a TEDx talk."

—Henkjan Smits, Trainer Business X-Factor, TEDxAmsterdam coach, Ambassador Sharing Success Foundation

ALSO BY JOJANNEKE VAN DEN BOSCH

So, You're An Orphan Now
Zo, nu ben je wees [Dutch]

LIVE YOUR TALKS

THE DIFFERENCE BETWEEN PUBLIC SPEAKING

AND PERFORMING AT A TEDx CONFERENCE

AND HOW TO OPTIMIZE YOUR OWN PRESENTATION

Publisher: Com Press by OnlineComm Academy
Strevelsweg 700-611, 3083 AS Rotterdam, Netherlands
+31 6 45110845

Copyright © 2016 by Jojanneke van den Bosch
All Rights Reserved.

The interviewed experts in this book may share their own (unaltered) interview in any way they see fit, provided that they mention the book title ('Live Your Talks' and its author (Jojanneke van den Bosch) and a clearly visible link to the website www.liveyourtalks.com.

No other parts of this book may be distributed in any way without written consent by the author. For questions or comments, please contact the publisher at www.onlinecomm.academy.

This book is not affiliated with TED.com or TEDx in any way. The contents of this book convey the personal experiences of the author while preparing for and performing at TEDxDelft.

Text: Jojanneke van den Bosch
Editor: Leah Krevit, USA

ISBN 9789082023282
First edition: March 2016

Cover, typesetting, visual quote design: OnlineComm Academy
Made print ready by Front-taal, Rotterdam
Photography: Winand Stut Photography, www.winandstut.nl
Printed in the Netherlands by Veenman+

For my father, Menno (1925 - 1989),
who could fill a room with himself and his stories.

For my mother, Aleida (1941 - 1990),
whose bright eyes, presence and temperament could outshine many.

For my foster dad, Coen (1945 - 2014),
my foster mom Marianne and my foster sister Eveline,
who have all taught me to be brave and to find home within.

For all my loved ones,
who are part of me and I of them.

JOJANNEKE VAN DEN BOSCH

LIVE YOUR TALKS

THE DIFFERENCE BETWEEN PUBLIC SPEAKING
AND PERFORMING AT A TEDx CONFERENCE
AND HOW TO OPTIMIZE YOUR OWN PRESENTATION

CONTENTS

Introduction	13
Live Your Talk	21
The Differences Between Business Presentations and TEDx talks	27
What A TEDx Talk Is And What It Is Not	39
Crafting Your Talk	49
Storytelling: Paint A Picture	57
What a TEDx Speaker Coach Tells You	71
Speaker Style: Connecting With Your Audience	83
Rehearsing Your Talk	103
Multimedia Shock Therapy, Or Is Less More?	111
Feedback	123
Emotions In Yourself And In Your Talk	135
Courage And Stage Fright	149
Showtime	177
After TEDx: Investing, Growing, Harvesting	197
Continuously Reinventing Yourself In Public Speaking	211
Discover More	219
Thank You	223

INTRODUCTION

Dear You,

Maybe you picked up this book because you are a public speaker or because you want to perform more confidently. Perhaps you just love watching TED and TEDx talks, those inspiring talks that are being performed almost every single day, somewhere in the world. Perhaps you have attended a TED or TEDx conference. And perhaps you have even performed at one of the many TEDx stages and want to compare notes. Maybe you're dreaming of performing on cool big stages and you've even already written your thank you notes. Or maybe you don't know who this guy people call 'Ted' is and you're wondering what the fuss is about. In any case: thank you for reading this book. I appreciate it and I hope you find it to be useful and entertaining.

The question I hear most regarding my performance at TEDxDelft is 'How did you get on that stage? Did you apply or were you invited?'.

Many people consider performing at a TEDx conference as some kind of academic degree, an external confirmation of knowledge and skill. In some ways, it is. Far more importantly, it is a station. A stop on a track of a long journey. Not just towards it, but also with a long track afterwards. If you consider your life a long track with many stops, you see an array of expectations, wishes and ambitions. When these expectations, wishes and ambitions are a profound part of you, you're never 'stuck'. You are always able to look beyond any stop on your life track. There's a journey before a every stop, there's a story during a certain stop and there's a journey after every stop. It's up to you what kind of story your stop will be.

In this book, I share my experiences preparing my TEDx talk, the speech that changed the way I prepare for performances in general. I want you to benefit from my experiences and insights, whether you are actually invited to perform at a TEDx conference or not. I have found that preparing for a TEDx talk is entirely different from working on any other presentation or performance. Having been a seasoned public speaker for over ten years and having performed on corporate stages over three hundred times, I was very thankful to be given the opportunity to learn this. Because I got to learn something new. And I was completely open to the humbling experience.

There is nothing casual or easy about learning how to perform your best at a TEDx conference. It would be unreasonable if I (or any other TEDx performer for that matter) would casually toss in the TEDx talk in any conversation. If you see anyone being blasé about this, please know that deep in their hearts, they were incredibly nervous beforehand. This is also the case if they assure you that they 'just did it right and it felt comfortable'. These people know that you haven't seen them back stage. Trust me, we were all nervous back stage. All of us. And that's the right sentiment. It kept us focused and determined. And it created a bond, in a weird and positive way.

In the end, the bonus was doing the actual performance. The old saying 'It's about the road, not about the destination' in true in some ways. Not in every way, because the destination—the performance itself—really is the main goal. But the things I've learned and experienced are so valuable to me, that it would be downright greedy and selfish if I wasn't willing to share these insights with you.

VERBAL FAMILY
My mother and father both filled any room with their presence the moment they walked in the door. They were eloquent and they loved entertaining. My Dad's parents were born in the nineteenth century. They were true rhetoricians. During their time in college in Amsterdam, my grandparents participated in reciting contests. They recited medieval scriptures and pieces by Joost van den

Vondel and took pride in doing so without errors. And at our own home, birthdays were always animated verbal fests. Speaking was my parents' way. And it became my way.

Unfortunately, both my parents passed away prematurely in 1989 and 1990 and left me and my sister orphaned when I was fourteen years of age.

I'd like to share three experiences from my personal history in this introduction. Not to map out my resume, but to show you which three key moments triggered me to pursue the art of speaking in my career and life.

SPEAKING
In 1999, one year after my graduation from art school, one of my high school teachers with whom I am still connected after all these years, asked me to be the day presenter of the 50 year anniversary of the high school I had attended until 1993. This came as a surprise, since I had only attended the school the last eighteen months of my high school career (after my relocation to the other side of the country). So, my former teacher and mentor asked me to be the main presenter for this big event at this school where he had been a pupil himself, many decades ago. This was an honour. But I didn't understand. My teacher looked at me and said: "Listen. You have managed to finish high school despite the hardship you encountered at the time, after your parents passed away. You didn't think we, your teachers, didn't know about that? We believe you have a story to share. We'd like to hear how this was for you. Besides, I think that speaking in front of this strong community will be a good challenge for you. To be seen and...heard. I hear you still have that occasional stutter. Don't worry about it too much. You'll be fine. Oh, and please don't forget to mention all the people who receive credits. They're on the list."

This was an important lesson for me. Being asked to speak at the 50 year anniversary wasn't just an honour. It was a challenge. My former teacher and mentor was still teaching me. He wanted me to do even better. I took up that challenge. Did it go well? Yes. I shared one or two of my personal experiences of growing up without parents and going to school at the same time. There were even teachers in the room who wanted to talk to me after my presen- tation, teachers I hadn't connected with when I was still in high school. But did it go phenonenally well? Not by a long shot. I managed to forget to mention half of the list of important people I was told not to forget. My teacher was a bit put out by that. And for good reason. But that day, he taught me several great lessons.

The first lesson was: You may be the one speaking, but your message is not (and shoudn't be) about you. Secondly, don't mistake a challenge for an honour that's been granted to you. And finally, be open to feedback and always stay open to improvement of your skills.

You are never done, and that's a good thing. Even people with a stutter can grow to be public speakers. Forever cherish your mentors, for learning is one of the greatest gifts in life.

PERFORMING
Years later, I worked at a public housing corporation as a communication consultant where I coordinated projects focused on local housing development, economical impulse and techno- logy. We had been working very hard on one particular project. And our efforts paid off: one day, we were invited to present our innovative concept to the mayor and the city council. We had all hands on deck to make this an incredibly cool presentation. I had designed a booklet and a slide deck and I wrote speaker's notes to be able to address all possible questions correctly. I'd invited the press, prepared my talk and accomplished all things necessary. This day wouldn't be just about giving a presentation. It would be about proving that I had potential to do more than was included in my job description. I wanted to grab that moment. This was performing. I knew it!

The evening before the big day, my boss phoned me and said: "My job description says I am the spokesperson for the press and other external engagements. Give me your speaker's notes. I'll be presenting for the city council tomorrow." "Wait, what?" I replied. "But you haven't been in the project team and can't answer their questions. Do you expect this to work out?" "This is the way it's going to go. You give me your notes, and if they ask piercing questions, I'll just ask for a recess."

I replied: "Okay, I'll give you my notes. Let me add just two more words to them." I quit. This was the beginning of the creation of my business OnlineComm Academy in April 2006.

RESONATING

In 2005, I got my first chance to speak in front of an audience as a presenter at a conference about digital innovation in education. I was the substitute for the original presenter, who had called in sick. In the same year, I had crafted a workshop for my clients called 'Beamer Be Gone!' I had seen dozens of people making a mess of their opportunities to perform on stage. They were reading their cluttered slides out loud (hello, we can read). They were shining the back of their heads towards the audience. They often torpedoed enormous amounts of jargon, which annoyed or intimidated audience members more than it inspired them. Some people were just reading from a paper. Others winged it, but nobody knew what purpose their story had exactly. Glazed eyeballs stared back at the presenter, who was completely happy with his or her performance.

I'm not trying to trash any kind of style in public speaking. It's not my job to do so. Still, many of these unintended messes didn't have to happen. And with my workshop 'Beamer Be Gone,' I offered something that could change bad presentation habits of many speakers. It worked well. But if I were to develop the training all over again, I would change some things that I only discovered by completing this road I traveled.

INTERNALIZED INSIGHTS

These three events have helped me grow as a speaker and performer in my daily professional endeavours. I discovered that speaking, performing and resonating are HOW I do my job, regardless of WHAT the job is. Currently, my job is to make valuable online instruction from lessons I have learned, internalized and practiced, so that others can benefit from those lessons. That is the core of my 'body of work' and the purpose of my career. And yes, this book is part of this way of working: I teach what I have discovered, internalized and practiced about public speaking, so you can benefit from those insights. Furthermore, my company founded OnlineComm Academy, the first online learning platform in Europe with e-courses and blended learning programs about developing online strategy and mastering social media. It contains over twenty-five online courses. I mention this because the way I teach is verbal, for the most part. I use my voice to share ideas, insights and practical instructions, in videos, in livestream performances, on stage and in books. My words and my voice are my tools.

STEEP LEARNING CURVE
I may have been a public speaker for over ten years now, but when I started out, I also had a steep learning curve. I used to be what one calls 'a natural speaker who loves to improvise and thinks time is a relative concept'. I have worked hard to improve. I'm still a natural speaker and I still love improvising, but many things have changed in my way of performing over the years. Learning the art of performing a well crafted talk for a deserving audience has been a humbling experience and a blessing.

The art of presenting lies in your ability to share a story vividly and in a way that your audience can relate to, so your message resonates. It doesn't matter which topic—technology, entertainment, design, or puppy care—you cover, as long as you add something new to the equation, you entice people to engage in your story. Even if their engagement is just in their minds because verbal interaction with the audience and vice versa is prohibited during the presentation. You do the story justice and you make sure your message will resonate. You are the medium. The story is not your promotional instrument. This is a big differences between good presentations and great presentations.

So there are good and great presentations. And yes, 'good' and 'great' are vague qualifications. A great wedding speech is not the same as a great State Of The Union. But in the heart of the one performing the speech, it is. And it should be. So always aim to improve your abilities, no matter the purpose of your presentation. 'Good' and 'great' are relative qualifications in all stages of learning the craft of public speaking. We'll just have to be more specific about what 'good' and 'great' mean to us individually. And, more importantly, to your audience. If you're just speaking for yourself, you have no business performing. Because let's face it, you are not speaking for yourself. You are speaking to help other people a little bit further along the way. And if that's your goal, you better perform well.

In this book, I share happy as well as excruciating moments I experienced while preparing for my TEDx talk, and practical tips and insights that may come in handy for your own performance. An excellent team of experts was willing to share their insights and experiences in interviews. I am deeply grateful for their stories, and to you, for reading this. I hope you find my story, insights and tips useful and entertaining.

Speak, perform, resonate!

Jojanneke van den Bosch, March 2016

If it needs
my mind,
heart and hands,
it is worth
my voice.

LIVE YOUR TALK

Hello TEDx

On a regular working day in April 2014, I received an email from one of the TEDxDelft curators. "We'd like to meet you. We might be interested in inviting you to speak at our TEDx conference." I stared at the screen.

TEDx. Really? Now that was a stage I was excited about. And impressed with.

I welcomed the curators to my office and we talked about lots of things: Life, work, trying to make a difference, history, places, wishes, online communication, social media, innovations in e-learning. There were various topics in my professional and personal life that I wanted to share. At first, it wasn't at all clear what my talk would be about. If you're working on diffcrent topics in your career, you know that you will have to choose one, and only one, for a presentation. During this conversation, we trimmed all the topic options down to just one theme. It was the theme I wanted to explore and share with an audience. This is the most important question for selecting a topic to speak about at a TEDx conference. Ask yourself: What is the single most important idea I want to share with the world?

The hours wooshed away as we enjoyed pots of coffee and got to know each other a little better. When we said goodbye, I felt exhilarated and inspired. I knew I'd met some amazing people. That would be true, no matter what the committee's decision.

After several weeks, I smiled at my inbox. "We're glad to inform you that you have been selected to perform at TEDxDelft on February 27th 2015" the message read. Whoa!

I signed a contract in which I swore to be silent until January 2015, when the publicity roller coaster would start. It felt like a happy little secret I carried with me. It was something I cherished and I was absolutely determined to be well-prepared for the TEDx stage. My boyfriend was the only one I shared this information with. There was more than enough time to prepare for the talk. Nine months. It felt as if I was pregnant. And in a way, I was.

TED and TEDx talks were my standard go-to place on YouTube. I had been watching them during hours of procrastination, rainy Sunday afternoons and during lunch breaks. My friends and I shared links to talks that had captivated us. We wanted them to reach greater audiences. We all were watching these talks, during good times and not so good times. Most times, they lifted my spirits and made me feel connected to my goals and dreams and to a better world in general. Sometimes, they touched a vulnerable place in my heart. And now I was granted the opportunity to do something like that for others. This came as a surprise and it was an incredible gift. The following two months I became a bit more used to the idea and I planted the seeds of what would eventually become my talk.

After pondering which topic I wanted to cover (innovation in e-learning was the obvious choice), I decided I would talk about how I grew up after my parents died and how I eventually found a good path in life, thanks to my foster parents, Marianne and Coen. The decision was clear and it gave me peace of mind. I was totally going to do this. And I wanted to do it differently from other talks I had seen about overcoming hardships. I had shared my story in my book 'So, You're An Orphan Now', and I wanted more people to know about the struggles that orphans in the Western world experience and how we can help them build a better life for themselves. There was no reason to hold back now. So I planned my summer break, celebrated my thirty-ninth birthday on midsummer's day, and continued helping my e-learning students and corporate clients. And I continued crafting my talk.

One deceptively sunny Saturday morning in July, the phone rang. My foster mother Marianne was calling. She and my foster dad had just returned home from their holiday trip to Ireland.

"Coen is terminally ill and only has a few months to live."

KEY TAKEWAYS

Life is what happens while...

I was working on a story that was supposed to be complete, but was actually still developing. One of the most important people in my talk, my foster dad, was walking the roughest journey of his life, the one towards his own death. This was a journey that he could only walk by himself. And there I was, creating my path to TEDx. He was letting go of his precious life, while I was writing the narrative of how he had saved me and taught me how to build a better life for myself. He had empowered me, but now he had to come to terms with his own untimely death.

The oath of secrecy
The moment I signed the TEDx contract, I had agreed to all the terms. One of these terms was that I wouldn't be allowed to tell other people (until a particular date, eight months from the signing of the contract) that I was going to perform at a TEDx conference. Actually, I cherished the confidentiality. It kept me safe from influences from the outside world. No judgments, no expectations, no questions asked. The agreement provided me with the freedom to let my story mature in the most pure and protected way possible. The secret was safe with me, as was the story.

The moment I heard about my foster dad being terminally ill, I stopped working on my presentation. The contrast felt too confronting. The presentation seemed almost banal in comparison. This situation felt like the "ultimate of relativity". The talk was important to me, but my foster dad had an importance that exceeded any accomplishment that I could ever achieve. I was thinking a lot about life. Life is not about achievement. You can achieve things in life, as long as you're alive. But life itself is a completely different matter. Life has been given to you. You didn't create it.

I believe that we are the ones that have to find meaning in our own lives. And now I had to come to terms with this idea once more, in real time. While I was writing the presentation, I was—once more—experiencing the fragility of life.

My foster dad had a hard time in accepting his approaching untimely death. He had always been a proud man, a strong man, who had served his country for many years. Accepting weakness and this ruthless vulnerability was a struggle for him and his loved ones. He chose to deal with the first emotions by himself. This meant that many family members, including me, didn't know whether or not we would ever talk to him or see him again. This was intensely emotional for everyone involved. For at least a week, I could barely function due to grief. After about ten days, I picked up where I left off in writing my speech. The blessing in disguise was that I discovered right then and there that the story I wanted to share was the right one. It would not only become a well-deserved tribute to one of the people who had given me a sense of security in my life when I was a sixteen year old girl. It would also be a gift. His good deeds could become an inspiring and practical example of what anyone could do when encountering a young person struggling to find their way in life. This was my way of giving meaning to the ruthless fact that Coen wasn't going to be with us much longer. And it gave me the motivation to make it the best speech I could ever give.

Speaking at TEDx is as much about you learning a lot as it is about you teaching things.

THE DIFFERENCES BETWEEN BUSINESS PRESENTATIONS AND TEDX TALKS

The Idea I Wanted To Share More Than Anything

While the TEDxDelft curators and I were discussing over pots of coffee which topic I would address, my foster dad was already ill. And nobody knew. Ironically, I had to prepare myself for giving THE talk I wanted to share with the whole world, while my foster dad faced his own untimely demise.

The first week after I heard about his illness, I didn't touch anything concerning my talk. Knowing about the upcoming intense loss of one of my most important role models filled me with grief and stirred emotions as if they were whirling in a snow globe. The echo of the losses I would be speaking about were resonating in my present; I was losing another parent. If you know the story of Harry Potter: Coen was my Sirius Black.

The talk I was preparing wouldn't be the first time that I had shared the story about how I grew up without my parents. I had talked about that in my first book 'So, You're An Orphan Now', on the radio, in a documentary on national television, in newspaper and magazine interviews. But it would be the first time that I had to distill my experiences down to a talk of eighteen minutes, with a small selection of true stories that would illustrate the core message that I was trying to express. Nothing more, nothing less. I wanted to reach the core of the message and find a way to make it 'portable' for my audience.

The fact that I had lived through the story myself was not the reason the message was so crucial.

The primary reason I wanted to address this. I couldn't remain silent about this, knowing that to do otherwise would make me an accomplice to the misery of today's orphaned children.

I wanted to help make an inevitable and unstoppable change in theirlives. Many of these children are struggling every day, living with grief for the loss of their parents. Struggling to pay the rent. Struggling to find a job, to go to school, and trying so hard to go on, every day. Living your life without your parents can often be more like a survival challenge than it is living a life. Surviving isn't the equivalent of living. I know that first hand. I felt I couldn't look the other way when I'd see other young people struggling to build a better life. And these orphaned children are in great numbers: every day, somewhere in the world, 5,760 children lose their parents. So awareness was key. The next step was: inspiring adults to notice these children, provide them with a short-term solution and empowering them to build a better life for themselves. Sharing on this international platform was necessary to raise awareness about orphaned children in my country and in other Western countries. The goal was clear. But where to start?

The difference between corporate presentations and TED or TEDx talks is a big one. This difference is very significant to me. One is not better than the other. But they are two very different kinds of talks. Since I had already explored this topic in my first book and in the media. I had to make the translation to TEDx. I came up with a key that worked like a charm for me:

A business presentation is a talk you have to do and you want to perform as best as humanly possible.

A TEDx talk is THE talk you want to share with the whole world before you can die in peace. It contains an idea that makes your story unique and entices people to act differently. Knowing and believing this is the best place to start writing your "idea worth spreading."

I knew what to do.

KEY TAKEWAYS

A New Perspective On Something You Thought You Knew…

If you have viewed TED or TEDx talks on YouTube or at a conference, you've probably noticed that the topics aren't limited to certain areas. The three main TED concepts are Technology, Entertainment and Design. This covers a lot of ground. These talks differ greatly from business presentations that may or may not be about technology, entertainment or design. So, what is the difference between TEDx talks and business talks? If it isn't the choice of topic, could it be in the way the stories are delivered? That is indeed a factor. But the key factor that distinguishes TED and TEDx talks from other types of talks is that they convey an "idea worth spreading."

All TED and TEDx talks are created around a concept, an idea, that entices you to look at this particular topic from a new perspective. Some of the TED and TEDx talks are about inventions most of us never knew anything about. Other talks trigger us to take a new perspective on something we already have an opinion or a fair amount of knowledge about.

Some corporate talks may have this quality as well, particularly when the message is about vision, changing a strategic course, or similar themes. But usually, corporate talks are about informing collegues or stakeholders about project updates and financial quarterly statements. They might be inspiring talks about new developments in a business niche. They don't always carry an idea worth spreading. A new or different idea is not necessarily a novelty, but it can force you to change perspective, to think about what you thought was true before you were confronted with this new perspective.

Deliverance
And then there's the issue of choosing the right way to present this idea. I had given over three hundred presentations before TEDxDelft. But I knew there would be challenges during rehearsals. Your natural style usually does not fit the TEDx concept completely. You'll have to adjust to the style and nature of the conference, without neglecting your own personal style. To make a long story short: you have to improve your skills, no matter how experienced you may be.

What not to do
Most people who have taken a course in presenting already know these fatal errors: Inflicting death by PowerPoint. Reading slides (worst case: turning your head while reading and showing the audience the back of your head). Speaking in a monotone voice. Making little if any eye contact. Drowning people in information, data and facts. Ingnoring the audience's needs. Telling bad jokes. Laughing at your own bad jokes. Being boring.

And yet, so many presenters still do these things.

There is hope
The TEDx format prevents these errors from occurring in several different ways. First and foremost, the presenter must present his or her story to their TEDx curators and speaker coach, before they even get the chance to mess it up. That's good news. Furthermore, once you are invited to speak at a TEDx conference, chances are that you watched other people's TED and TEDx performances and concluded that you don't want to do your usual schtick the way you once did in front of a corporate board. And last, the stage manager checks out your slide deck (if you even need one). But that doesn't mean that you're in the safety zone.

Difference 1: The audience wants to soak up every word
Attending a TEDx talk is something really wonderful. You're in this packed room, and everyone around you, just as yourself, has an insatiable craving for new ideas, for inspiration, for connection.

Every single person around you wants you to succeed. Everyone's rooting for you. They attend a TEDx event because they want to be surprised and want to experience new ideas about an array of topics.

Maybe this sounds slightly odd, but this differs a great deal from other huge, corporate style conferences with thousands of people in the room that have paid top dollar (or got a free ticket from their boss to go do some networking on behalf of the company). At those events, chances are just a small part of the crowd is rooting for you to perform your best. They probably have been scrolling through the event website, looking for the most relevant presentation titles for their business. Some talks will even be skipped because the networking talks during the coffee breaks were just too promising.

Difference 2: There's no product, there is only your core message
Every single attendee at a TEDx conference, and everyone who is watching TEDx talks on YouTube on a regular basis, knows that there is no product sold in any TEDx talk. Any TEDx talk evolves around an idea, a concept, an invention or a new insight. In corporate talks, you might present a quarterly financial statement, or the pros of a new product or a new project. You might even say that if a corporate talk lacks a certain financial or educational angle or product pitch, it hasn't got a right to be presented in a corporate setting. This is a big difference in purpose.

Difference 3: Customizing your presentation style for TEDx
Over the years, I've developed a certain presentation style that reflects my knowledge level and personality. I've integrated my talents and learnings in my presentation style, so that I can tap into them any time I'm in front of an audience. I won't say I have a particular routine, but there are certain elements in my presentation that make it a distinct Jojanneke-style experience. You might say that it's my personal signature. Having a personal touch in your presentation is a powerful and convenient asset. However, you might have to slightly alter your presentation habits when you're invited to perform at a TEDx conference.

It's just not something you can improvise too much. Nor can you wing it on the basis of a few keywords. It just won't be enough.

Difference 4: Money
One obvious difference between public speaking and speaking on a TEDx stage is the speaking fees. Most public speakers are accustomed to receiving fees for their performances. If you are invited to perform at TEDx, you don't get paid for it financially.

Many professional speakers critique the organization's policy not to pay speakers, because public speaking is indeed a profession. It is a skill mastered over a significant period of time and advanced skills are worth every penny. As much as I agree with this latter concept (I also usually do not work for free), I do agree with the policy about not being paid for a TEDx performance. In my point of view, TED and TEDx are amazing opportunities to share your "idea worth spreading." The vast majority of ideas worth spreading are not a hundred percent translatable to cash. And I think that's a good thing. Because most important things in life are not about money.

Sometimes money is the hurdle to change the world and to get the idea worth spreading across. Hurdles can be a nuisance. And in the case of TEDx, removing the hurdle meant removing the money. When the stage is not about money but instead about core values, the risk of the ideas worth spreading on stage being blurred by economic intentions is radically minimized. And this is as it should be. I wouldn't want to pitch my product in my carefully crafted idea worth spreading. It would not only come across as strategic marketing, but selling anything other than your pure message would tarnish the pureness of it.

There's nothing wrong with marketing. I love marketing. It's part of my job. There's nothing wrong with selling. I love selling. We do it every day. That's the core of any business. If you don't sell anything, you're not in business.

But TEDx isn't a business. It's a non-profit.

The money issue

If your purpose is 'pitching an idea to directly convert it financially', the TEDx stage is not for you. That's not necessarily a bad thing. There are heaps of opportunities for you to pitch ideas and products, share them with the world, and convert them into a buck or two. For instance: you could speak at in-company inspiration sessions. You could apply as a speaker to upcoming conferences in your country (you won't always be asked to perform and you don't have to feel ashamed for asking to participate). You could organize an event about your expertise and product line and invite yourself and other experts in your field as speakers. You could offer to speak at meetings of business clubs.

There really are loads of ideas for getting more speaking gigs in the business world.

But as far as TEDx is concerned, I feel completely comfortable not being paid for my performance. It was an honour and privilege to be given the opportunity to learn something new and to share the message that I want the whole world to hear and internalize. Besides not getting paid, preparing for my talk has cost me a considerable amount of money, because I decided to decline more than one rather lucrative project for my business in order to make enough time to prepare for this talk. I feel it's been worth every single penny. I'm not saying that every TEDx speaker should choose to decline lucrative projects. It was my call and if I were to do it all over again, I would make the same decision in a heartbeat.

Pros And Cons

The fact that TED and TEDx don't pay speakers is something many speakers have various opinions about. If you do a quick search on Twitter or Google with the keywords 'pay', 'speakers' plus 'TEDx', you get a glimpse of the palet of opinions. I'll give you a few examples. On his blog, Frank Swain (https://medium.com/futures-exchange/why-im-not-a-tedx-speaker-3be652b8eccb#.ihfyodbq8) shares that he has been invited to speak at a TEDx conference, but declined because of the no payment rule. He feels that talent always has to be paid and that the TED organization makes lots of money, so not paying speakers would be unfair, in his opinion. Jayson Elliot replied to Swain's statement on his blog (http://jaysonelliot.com/blog/2013/11/18/why-you-shouldnt-be-paid-to-speak-at-ted/), by emphasizing that TED and TEDx can attract immensely famous people and visionaries as well as people who haven't been in the limelight, but do have new visions and ideas. He writes on his blog: "Some of the people who speak at TED are luminaries of the highest order. Bill Gates, Al Gore, J.J. Abrams, Bono, Oliver Sacks, Bill Joy, Jane Goodall...show me a conference that could afford to pay the speaking fees such giants might command. By paying no one, the conference can attract talent at all levels, and presumably can also avoid the politics and bad feelings that would come with negotiating the cost of, say, a Malcolm Gladwell vs. a Tony Robbins or a Seth Godin."

It goes without saying that I respect all opinions on this issue. For me personally, it hasn't been a dilemma at all. I just wanted to share my idea with the world more than anything, because I felt (and still feel) that it's worth spreading and because my idea can change the lives of orphaned children in the Western world. If you perform well and your talk resonates with your audience, you have a bigger chance at getting paid events, as you may already have been before. And for the record and in general, though, I do not believe it should be a habit of event managers not to pay its speakers. Speaking is a discipline. It's a job that you have been working on improving for years. If you have value to share, than it should be rewarded accordingly, financially and otherwise.

When I started out as a speaker in 2004, I sometimes received invitations to speak at events where my target group wouldn't even be in attendance. The organizers usually said something like "you won't get paid, but it's worth the network opportunites; you'll get to know people who might want to work with you!" Of course, this usually wasn't the case, because my target group wasn't even in the room. Nevertheless, I agreed up to twice a year to speak at those events, just to flex my presentation muscles, as well as to feel the joy of connecting people and knowledge, even though

I knew I wouldn't get anything out of it. That's also why I speak at universities and social-oriented organizations twice a year. No more, because time is the most valuable thing I 'have'. Other companies and clients pay my fee because the quality is worth their (and my) time. But after those two free speaking engagements, my calendar is not available for free rides. I value my quality and I teach my clients how to treat me and my products and services.

Difference 5: Personal purpose
When you give a corporate talk, it is usually part of your job. Perhaps you love doing it, perhaps you don't. There are various reasons to perform in corporate contexts. You might strive to achieve that promotion, or to develop your skills so other people notice you and your talents, or to educate colleagues.

But when you give a TEDx talk, another dynamic is in play. During (or even before) crafting and practicing such a talk, many TEDx speakers discover just how determined they are. Some can't imagine themselves years from that moment, regretting they didn't do that big talk. I believe that regretting something you never did is worse than regretting (or even being thrilled about) something you did do. I'm not talking about performing at a TEDx conference per se, but rather sharing your insight with the world in any significant way that's available to you. This sharing creates something meaningful in your life. It may be just one of many meaningful things in your life. But I think striving for meaning, whether it be personal or professional, is more important than exhibiting your professional knowledge for your day job. That of course is my personal opinion.

The World of Professional Speaking
Public speaking is a profession. There are many people who dedicate their careers to performing in front of audiences. They share their expertise about their subject as effectively and eloquently as they can. They improve their performance every day. They learn and perfect their craft every single day. They are connected internationally through speakers associations, such

as the Global Speakers Federation and their locally affiliated societies in many countries. They follow the key competencies that the National Speakers Association has defined: Eloquence, Expertise, Enterprise and Ethics.

There are also many speakers who speak in front of audiences because it is part of their jobs. For instance, communication consultants, management specialists, researchers and innovators and teachers who share their insights and expertise. It's part of the work they do on a daily basis. However you choose to integrate all these points of advice about speaking, keep one thing in mind; be yourself. Please don't change into some corporate tiger if you weren't one before, when you find yourself in front a a boardroom or TEDx audience. Aiming to be the best version of who YOU can possibly be is your safest bet in the long run. This also increases the chance that your message will come across the way YOU want it to.

The World of TED and TEDx: the culture, the purpose
The TED concept was launched by graphic designer Richard Saul Wurman in 1984. The letters TED stand for Technology, Entertainment and Design. Wurman started TED by inviting collegues from Apple, Adobe, IBM and the Hollywood film industry to exchange ideas. After the millennium switch, media entrepreneur Chris Anderson took over TED. From that moment on, TED became known as THE conference where "ideas worth spreading" were presented. In 2006, the talks were also published online. The conference blueprint remained intact: every presenter got a maximum of eighteen minutes to make his or her point and it was not possible to have any kind of verbal interaction with the audience. The eighteen minute limit proved to be powerful and effective. Surely, if you can't make your point in a few minutes, you don't have a point.

TED talks inspired so many people and became so incredibly popular, that in 2009 it became possible to organize TED-like conferences in every other part of the world. TEDx was born. In the Netherlands, the country I live in, a smart and ambitious man called Jim Stolze, founded TEDxAmsterdam. He had already climbed the TED stage in California. TEDxAmsterdam was an instant success. Jim Stolze has written a book about the economy of attention, in which he shares how he performed for TED and how he founded TEDxAmsterdam. After Amsterdam, more cities in the Netherlands followed. My talk was at TEDxDelft, at Delft, University of Technology.

Rules
It is not uncommon for presenters to feel stifled by the amount of rules and regulations they receive prior to their talk (at various events, not just TEDx). "You must stay on the red dot." "Ask three people in the audience a question." "Reserve 7 minutes for Q&A". And so on. If you are trying to honour all reasonable and unreasonable requests, you might find yourself struggling with your core message, your own presentation style and even your own high standards. From my point of view, it can be quite liberating if you bend the rules a little.

Always remember that the person or company who invites you to speak wants to give you the opportunity to present your message in the most effective and convincing way YOU can. There is, however, one big catch: make sure not to drown your audience in information from a desire to be complete in the delivery of your story. You should tell them exactly what they need to know that will make a difference to their lives or business. Make sure you have all the information, data and supporting evidence available, but don't dump it all on them like snow in Aspen. Your job is to be clear, concise, and compelling. So stay focused on everything they need to know, not what you'd like them to know because you've worked so hard on it. Your presentation is about the message you want to deliver. It's not about how much you know. It's about what they need to know. That's the catch.

As far as the unnecessary rules are concerned, take more space if you need it. If you don't want to use (or don't need) slides, don't use one. If you want to ask one person in your boardroom a question, do that. Perhaps the only 'rule' you'd like to honour is standing on that dot, if it's a TED or TEDx dot. In all other cases: BE the dot.

Stay focused on everything they need to know, not what you'd like them to know, just because you've worked so hard on it.

Your presentation is about the message you want to deliver. It's not about how much you know. It's about what they need to know.

WHAT A TEDX TALK IS AND WHAT IT IS NOT

Taking On The Challenge

The TEDxDelft team was professional and very experienced. TEDxDelft is the second TEDx organization after TEDxAmsterdam. TEDxDelft had organized several TEDx conferences, and also initiated TEDxDelftSalon, and later also TEDxDelftWomen. The way the curators had approached and interviewed me gave me a feeling of reassurance: these people wanted to be absolutely confident they were making the right decision. They raised the bar and I gave it my best. They provided me with two speaker coaches, gave me a clear oversight on the TEDx regulations and advice for speakers, and helped me to decide on the scope of my topic.

I was accustomed to giving presentations. By this point, I had given over three hundred of them. I had covered various topics, mainly about online communications, social media, and e-learning, but also my personal experiences as an orphaned child. I was familiar and comfortable with my topics. But bringing my story to the TEDx format was something much more challenging than I had imagined before I began writing and rehearsing the talk.

The first thing I thought was: How on earth am I going to choose which stories I'll skip? There was just so much to tell. I wanted to be complete, but also nuanced. That was a trap. There is room for nuance in a TEDx talk, but the message has to be razor sharp.

I had to 'crunchify' the story nuggets and make them carry the message. This meant I had to start with a first draft and then kill darlings. I killed many. My first draft was a bloody battlefield.

After writing my first draft, I read the piece out loud and timed myself. It took me forty-three minutes. Seriously. Not a joke. I knew my pitfall was being somewhat prolix. I had inherited that from my father. My father Menno was a creative and witty man.

But he couldn't tell a joke in, give or take, under an hour and a half. It was amusing in the end, but while he was telling a joke, usually people in the room were uncomfortably wiggling in their chairs, looking frantically for ways to escape. My dad may have been funny, but wasn't particularly good at telling jokes. Sometimes my mother would walk in the room, revealing his carefully crafted punch line. Brutal, but also funny. But my dad excelled in telling stories and writing poems and was the most enthusiastic man you'd ever meet. It appeared that I had inherited my dad's vice of being too lengthy in my talks. It was obvious I had to delete lots and lots (and lots) of unnecessary sentences, nuances and examples. It took me weeks (again, not kidding) to delete enough copy to get me in the safety zone of eighteen-ish minutes. My speaker coaches were grateful that I didn't rob them of any more time than necessary. They also—wisely—told me that there would be zero room for improvisation. This prevented me from stepping into the obvious trap.

The beginning of this process taught me the difference between telling stories, giving presentations and a TEDx talk.

Another difference between TEDx talks and other talks was something I instantly felt comfortable with. It resonated completely with the reason I had shared my story in my first book, two years prior to giving my talk: sharing the story wouldn't and shouldn't be about courage or 'just' sharing a vulnerable story. It had to be crafted to illustrate a core message. In my case, it was educating the audience, making them aware, and persuading them to act differently after leaving the event. Everything I did was with that goal in mind.

I can't emphasize enough the importance of only sharing stories that illustrate your "idea worth spreading." Leave all unnecessary stories out.

KEY TAKEAWAYS

Releasing Unnecessary Burden

Once you know that you probably have to kill practically all of your darlings (because that's usually what happens after writing your first draft), you might as well get into the process right away by asking yourself a few key questions: what is the essence of my idea worth spreading? What is new about it? Does it need a metaphor or story to illustrate it or to allow it to resonate with my audience? Does it provide my audience with something fresh and new? What do I want to change in my audience's behaviour once they leave the room after hearing the talk? Chances are that ALL the rest of your ideas will be deleted.

What a TEDx talk is: refreshing, confrontational, provides new insights or a new perspective on something you thought you already knew a lot about.

What a TEDx talk is not: It's Never, Ever Something Everybody Already Knew. It's not an organized group cheer for something somebody did. And a TEDx talk most definitely is not about you. It can refer to something you did or encountered, but the idea you're spreading is not about you as a person but about your message. Not about you. And it is never, ever a sales pitch. If you want to sell something, buy an ad or pitch at a business club.

"One of the best things
about attending a TEDx event
is that the program is so
carefully put together.

You're being thrown from the
left part of your brain
to the right part. This is done on
purpose, to provide you with a
feeling of being reset."

—Rob Speekenbrink

INTERVIEW

Rob Speekenbrink:

"As long as there are new ideas to discover, there will be room for TEDx"

Rob Speekenbrink is founder of TEDxDelft, European Ambassador for TEDx, and also founder and director at NosCura, Strategy & Implementation in Webcare and Online Content.

Rob, what was it that gripped you in the TEDx concept?
In my line of work, it's important to discover new things, get fresh ideas and get and stay inspired. To do so, I visit conferences and seminars, sometimes paying excessive fees. I have done so for years and years. At one point, I got tired of going to conferences while sometimes not even hearing truly new information. These events left me feeling annoyed and dulled. I started to feel robbed of my valuable time and was craving to be surprised in a positive way once more. One day, a friend introduced me to the TEDx concept. I agreed to attend TEDxRotterdam in the Nieuwe Luxor theatre. I was thrilled. Everything I heard and saw that day was completely new to me. It was invigorating, refreshing, inspiring and just wonderful. We looked at one another, and we had no idea why TEDx hadn't reached Delft yet, the city I live in.

Was the Delft, University of Technology on board as a host instantly or did you have to pull a lot of strings?
After attending TEDxRotterdam, I instantly decided to apply for the TEDx licence for Delft, with co-founder Simone De Jong. We built partnerships with TU Delft, University of Technology, my employer at the time, and with the municipality and local businesses. Everyone was enthusiastic and we found enough sponsors to make the first event work.

How did you create the curators group?
From the beginning, we curated all speakers ourselves. Simone and I asked Jeroen Van Erp to join us, so we'd have three people to select possible speakers for our conferences. Selecting with three people was essential, because if two people disagree about inviting or turning down a possible speaker, a third opinion is crucial to make a final decision. The third person always has the right to veto. This method works brilliantly for us. After some time, Simone chose another path in her career and we invited Caryn 't Hart de Wijkerslooth to join our team. The three of us decided to ask five friends to assist us with their critical opinions, because quality has always been our main priority. Also, extending our team, and with that our network, increased our chances of finding the perfect speakers for our conferences.

What are your most valuable lessons learned while organizing the TEDxDelft conferences?
Something always goes wrong, and you have to deal with that. It's such a special process. We work with lots of volunteers and professionals. Combining these two worlds this is challenging and intense. It's very worthwhile, and we couldn't make our conferences happen without these amazing people. As a conference licensee and manager, it can be somewhat awkward to claim someone's valuable time. You have to work with the available energy. And sometimes things go awry. We once had a situation in which one of the volunteers at that time wanted to be selected to perform at the TEDxDelft conference. This is against TED's and our regulations. Team members are strictly excluded from our speaker selection process.

What were the most astonishing messages your heard at TEDx conferences so far?
The mayor of Rotterdam, Mr. Ahmed Aboutaleb, expressed himself so openly and with so much honesty about his cultural background at the TEDxRotterdam conference. His performance resonated with me and the rest of the audience. And at our own TEDxDelft conference in 2012, seventeen year old Boyan Slat

made quite a lasting impression with his innovative idea and enthusiastic presentation. Both of these men radiated a sense of connection.

What do you love to see at TEDx conferences in the upcoming years?
I'd like to see a spin-off of TEDxDelft. Another event that connects content, people and ideas, but then about what happens after people have shared their idea worth spreading. In other words: what happens when an idea worth spreading has found its way in the world, and what concrete, tangible changes has this realized in the world? All those amazing new ideas that have made a difference in so many lives in so many countries. If one person can make a huge difference in one, two, two thousand or two million lives, what is the impact in the long run? How does people's behaviour change after learning something new? Wouldn't you just love to know? I would. It makes me extremely curious. That's on my bucket list. A What Happened After TEDx Conference. I can't wait to see this idea ignite.

Is there anything else you'd like to share?
The power of the TEDx concept is not in individual presentations. It's in the composition of the whole day. If someone knows TEDx just from watching the YouTube channels, I strongly advise them to go visit a real life TEDx event. It goes without saying that the YouTube channels are extremely valuable. That's a beautiful gift. You learn a lot from them, and every talk has been prepared with care. The YouTube channels open the door to learning more. But to be part of the magic of such an intense real life event is a special experience. You know that all speakers are doing their best to bring a compelling, new, fresh and intense story to this, for many intimidating, stage. These people often have rehearsed for months to present their message on that particular day. They have made sacrifices and are willing to stand there before you. There is such a dynamic during the event. One of the best things about attending a TEDx event is that the program is so carefully put together. You're being thrown from your left part of your brain

to the right part. This is done on purpose, to provide you with a feeling of being reset.

A while ago, I was walking in my home town, and two young men were talking about our conference. "Wait what, you were at TEDxDelft? Man, that is brilliant. How was it? I want to go too. You lucky bastard." "Yeah man." This filled me with a feeling of pride.

I realize however, that some TEDx events are better than others, for instance when it comes to speaker selection. This makes me sad. Poor selection procedures are usually the reason an event isn't as successful as it could have been. This is also why we sometimes read things online like: "We know that trick already." "We find new ideas on every corner of the street, and they don't always make it to TEDx." My thoughts about that last remark: as long as we don't know these undiscovered gems, there will be room and zest for a TEDx conference.

Many TEDx events do not meet the TEDx rules and regulations. This is one of the reasons I accepted a new role in the TEDx eco system. I have passed on my license for TEDxDelft to a suitable successor, and I will concentrate on quality standards for TEDx events in whole Europe. Jim Stolze, the wonderful man who brought TEDx to the Netherlands, is my predecessor. I take this role quite seriously.

What are the 5 absolute no-go's in the TEDx concept?
1.) Pitching your products or business. TEDx is not a commercial enterprise.
2.) Performing your usual schtick. We don't do that. We only want new ideas, presented in a way it suits the message.
3.) Adding all kinds of fluff to your performance. We just want to hear the story. So bring that the best way you possibly can. If the story is good enough, you won't need any support in terms of ballet dance groups, musicians or other additions. If those things are a part of your message, by all means, use them.

In which ways has being a TEDx licensee changed your life?
Hosting a TEDx conference is never a goal in itself. It is a way to do things that are interesting, fun and useful. And there are other ways to do what you really want to do. You don't need TEDx for that. It's 'just' a medium. But TEDx has undoubtedly opened doors for me. I have met interesting people, it has touched and changed my life. The same thing goes for the speakers. TEDx is one of the ways I can express myself creatively. It's a station on an ongoing journey. The train goes on. It always does. It stops at certain stations, where I meet new people on different platforms. People with new ideas. It's a journey all the same.

Creating your storyline takes time. Grant yourself the time you need to write the quality you are striving for.

CRAFTING YOUR TALK

Writing The Story While Living The Sequel

"Please. Please not Coen. Don't take him away from us. It's not fair. I can't believe it. This isn't happening. It can't be." Thoughts of disbelief, grief and anger whirled in my head and heart.

While I was choosing what I'd share, Coen was trying to come to terms with the fact that he'd only have a few more months to live. He chose to do that on solitude. I suppose you never really know how you'll deal with a medical message like that, until it happens to you. Coen didn't want to connect with anyone but his wife and daughter, my foster sister. I couldn't visit him, and his other family members couldn't either. Although we all respected his decision, I admit that it was painful at first. We didn't know whether or not we'd ever see him alive. This was difficult for me, of course because I loved and love him dearly, and also because I was writing about him. It was such a conflicted emotion: I was building up to a talk in which I shared the valuable things he had done for me, and he was trying to find a way to accept the fact that he was going to have to leave us all.

Coen was very good at living his life. He cherished life and all the wonderful things that came with it. He had enjoyed all good things in life. Vacations, family, love, hobbies, a meaningful career, friendships. Just before I heard about his fatal disease, I had sent him and his wife a postcard with a message ink stamped on it: 'The Best Things In Life Aren't Things'. We all agreed to that.

One of the walls in my living room was covered with pieces of paper, full of scribblings, key words and lots of drawn arrows. I was mindmapping my talk and deciding what I would share and what I would leave out. Ever since I studied graphic and interactive design at the art academy, I've started every creative project with mindmapping on paper. I wanted to see the talk, not just write it in words. Next, I distilled all those scribblings to a list of keywords that I organized in a pattern: introduction, the life-changing event, what happened afterwards, how many kids are in similar situations today (facts and figures), what did I need most, who did I meet, what did they change in my life, what are the three most important things I learned and how can the audience take these learnings to help today's kids build a better life for themselves.

In a nutshell, I was creating my storyline pattern.

Later, I integrated the metaphor of a girl walking a tight rope to illustrate how dangerous and insecure children feel when they have to take care of themselves, without their parents.

Once this storyline was clear, I started writing the first draft of my talk. My speaker coaches and director helped me to shorten the list of keywords that became the stepping stones in my talk. I started with a list of about thirty keywords, or stepping stones. Thirty was way too many. We first compressed them into twenty-five chunks, then fifteen, and then narrowed them down to ten. This was a crucial process of crafting and internalizing the talk and also a key part in rehearsing the performance.

Throughout the process of crafting the talk, I stayed open to ideas and suggestions my speaker coaches gave me. My only goal was to create the best talk possible, and I understood that nobody, not even trained storytellers and writers, can create a TEDx talk entirely by themselves. You need to embrace your team's expertise in order to get what you want.

During this preparation process, I was also working on other projects, like my presentations about e-learning innovation at Social Media Week Rotterdam. I instantly noticed that the preparation process with the cards had already changed the way I approached other speaking engagements. Refreshing!

KEY TAKEAWAYS

Overview In Mind During Times Of Turmoil

No matter what the circumstances while preparing your talk are; your sole purpose is to share an idea that is ready for the world. Whether it be on a TEDx stage or elsewhere. An idea that, after being spoken, is strong enough to stand on its own, even without you. To speak to inspire people in every corner of the world. Your message should contain a nugget of value that can change lives. This means that you have to maintain overview of your talk, the circumstances and your goal: performing well.

In a perfect world, and that's what we're striving for, your message should be something that touches you personally. If something moves you and has changed you and your perspective, chances are that you'll be able to bring this message forward effectively.

My personal mission was to profoundly change the way people perceive orphans and orphaned children in their own countries, cities and neighbourhoods, so that they would help them build a better life for themselves. This was my goal. I wasn't prepared to negotiate that, and I didn't have to. The challenge was to distill a message short and forceful enough to let it land properly. I reached this goal in the writing of the script.

Most presenting coaches advise you to adjust your talk to the niche of your audience. That's solid advice. But it doesn't work for TEDx conferences. You're not just talking to engineers or communicators or teachers or healthcare professionals. You are talking to people from your whole community, from many different backgrounds and educational levels. And afterwards, you are talking to everyone who watches TEDx channels on YouTube. That's basically everyone who is willing to explore and learn something new. That's not a niche. So make sure you do not use professional jargon that someone from another niche won't understand. At the same time, it's vitally important that you don't underestimate your audience. There are few things more annoying than someone who talks to you as if you were a child. The challenge in this is to

Have the guts to stick
to only one example,
if this example is strong
enough to carry your story.
Avoid over-complicating
things for your audience
(but never underestimate
their intelligence).

focus on your message and choose a great story arc with a piercing theme that anyone can relate to. Reel them in that way.

Structure

There are principles you can use to build a structure in your talk. One classic schematic that many people use works like this: You set the scene for what you're trying to say. This is an introduction in which you create the setting of the story. Then, you share the key message. The next phase is to elaborate on why this key message is true, by discussing three revealing questions and then adding facts and figures to support these three issues. Then you finish up by repeating the key message.

Classic story schematics might work like a charm in corporate settings, but I can assure you that the TEDx and TED organizers, curators and speaker coaches know all these schematics by heart, and see right through them, often by the time you have uttered your first three sentences.

TEDx audiences want to be surprised. Telling a captivating story and disrupting storyline schematics can be much more effective for you than slightly adjusting a corporate presentation.

A storyline schematic that TED and TEDx speakers have used is the classic Hero's Journey, which goes something like this: First, the story opens in the setting of the hero's everyday life. Then, the adventure begins. This usually means that the hero is being challenged with a problem that he has to solve. The hero feels afraid. Then the hero meets someone, a mentor if you will, who inspires him to go ahead and solve the problem. The hero takes up the challenge and gives it his best shot. Of course, this isn't going to be easy, and many hardships have to be overcome during his challenge. Then, finally, a pivotal event occurs and the hero succeeds in accomplishing his main goal. He returns back to his normal life and shows the world what he has learned, inspiring others so they can improve their own lives and have adventures, too!

The TED talks of Tyler Cowen ('Be Suspicious Of Simple Stories'), Joe Sabia ('The Technology Of Storytelling') and Andrew Stanton ('The Clues To A Great Story') may inspire you to take a more creative approach in crafting your story. Staying curious while crafting your talk is essential, in my opinion. There may be unexpected gems you hadn't even thought about while you were deciding on your topic. Exploring your story elements may reveal valuable data, such as methaphors you might use in your slide deck or different examples you might choose for your audience.

Context
If your talk is going to be about adding a new context or meaning to an existing concept, a vital element in your talk should be emphasizing a gap in knowledge. Chances are your audience already has a certain level of knowledge about one (or both) areas you are going to be discussing in your talk. To avoid any kind of eyeball-rolling in your audience, you should reveal what the key problem is in your thesis. Once you've gotten that out of the way, you can come up with your unique solution, which consists of one or more elements that the audience is probably already familiar with.

For instance, let's take a look at Edward Valstar's talk 'Joined At The Hip'. The core problem that he wants to address in his talk is the erosive material that artificial hips are made of. The solution to the problem consists of two elements and the audience knows about one of these elements, for certain. The first element: using liquid concrete to fix something indefinitely. The second element: medical operation techniques. Once you combine these two elements, the audience can accept the solution for the main problem (to see the final result of this solution and Edward's TEDx talk, please search for 'TEDxDelft' and 'Edward Valstar' on YouTube).

Bridge a gap
You have to bridge a gap in knowledge. It's essential. This bridge may consist of facts, figures, or an illustrative example. One of the most successful talks to use statistics in a illustrative and vivid way is Hans Rosling's talk 'The Best Stats You've Ever Seen'. The talk was so appealing to the imagination that Rosling's other "ideas worth spreading" also reached the TED stage. And that's not only a huge accomplishment, it's also proof that taking the

effort to load the value of your idea in an imaginative way will take you places. Have the guts to stick to only one example, if this example is strong enough to carry your story. Avoid over-complicating things for your audience (but please never underestimate their intelligence).

One of the most hilarious TED talks I've ever seen is 'How To Sound Smart In Your TEDx Talk'. It's carefully crafted by Will Stephen for TEDxNewYork. His entire talk seemed to be about nothing but the way that he is performing on a TEDx stage. But in fact, his talk was about something very useful: he showed the audience what the structure of many TEDx talks is by talking in that very same format, and performing in a way that many TEDx speakers do. Will Stephen studied communications skills, and that's exactly what he showed in the most entertaining way, with a lot of hand gestures, variation in vocal timbre, functional silences and statistics that look smart on his slide deck but have no significant meaning at all.

Stephen said things like: "I have absolutely nothing to say whatsoever. And yet, through my manner of speaking, I will make it seem like I do. Like what I'm saying is brilliant." And: "Now, I'm going to get started with the opening. I'm going to make a lot of hand gestures, I'm going to do this (wave) with my right hand. I'm going to do this (wave) with my left. I'm going to adjust my glasses. And then I'm going to ask you a question. By a show of hands, how many of you all have been asked a question before?"Hilarious. He proceeds: "See? If feels like it might make sense, doesn't it? Like maybe, just maybe, I'm building to some sort of satisfying conclusion. I mean, I'm gesticulating as though I am. I'm pacing, I'm growing in intensity, I'm taking off my glasses, which by the way, are just frames. I wore them to look smart, even though my vision is perfect." Watch the whole clip on YouTube. It's useful and amusing.

Get Your Facts Right

Do not ever try bluffing your way through a TEDx talk. The facts that you are stating to support your idea should be checked and rock solid.

Do not ever try bluffing your way through a TEDx talk. The facts that you are stating to support your idea should be checked and rock solid.

STORYTELLING: PAINT A PICTURE

Contemplative Summer

"I am tired, I feel sad because of Coen, I work too hard and my cat is ill. This whole summer sucks."

It's safe to say that my thoughts hadn't been on creating my talk in the weeks after we found out about my foster dad's condition. To make matters worse, the world seemed to be stuck in the centre eye of a storm twister. The Dutch plane MH-17 had been shot down by a BUK missile from Ukraine and our whole nation went into mourning. The only sentence I wrote down was: "You can't see it coming, but when it's there, everything changes."

Looking back, I see why I couldn't find words to describe my talk at that moment. There were just too many intense distractions that deserved one hundred percent of my attention. So I decided to write Coen a letter. It was the only thing I could do. The letter to Coen deserved my words.

At the end of that summer, in September, a documentary about how I had grown up without my parents aired national television. It had been recorded in April of the same year. As a complete surprise, the television crew had called my foster parents to be in the documentary as well. This had resulted in an emotional moment in the documentary. It was so special that they had driven for hours to be there for me. It was a very special surprise. During recording the documentary, we didn't know yet about Coen's illness. When it aired in September, it was special to see him in it, and I felt intensely grateful for having him and his wife and daughter in my life. I felt a shifting perspective within. Yes, I still felt intense grief about his expected untimely demise. Feelings of gratitude and pride were equally present. They helped me to refocus on writing. I didn't only want to feel proud of him. I wanted him to be proud of me also. Words returned to me. Clear, concise. No unnecessary bells and whistles.

Using language in your presentation you would normally not use comes across as affected, overacted and unnatural.

Telling a story is not just about choosing the right words and bringing them into the right order. It's also about choosing the way you present your story.

KEY TAKEWAYS

Be Mindful Of Your Choice Of Words

John Lennon once said: "When you're drowning, you don't think "I would be incredibly pleased if someone would notice I'm drowning and come and rescue me." You just scream."

Your choice of words is very important and has consequences for your story, your performance and for the way your audience will welcome what you share. Using language in your presentation you would normally not use comes across as affected, overacted and unnatural. Telling a story is not just about choosing the right words and bringing them into the right order. It's also about choosing the way you present your story. It's not without reason that you often hear that someone will perform at TEDx rather than present at TEDx.

When you present a story, you are not part of the story itself. You are the one who brings it. When you perform a story, the way you share your story, including your behaviour and choices on stage, add to the experience of the story for your audience. Perhaps you use props. Perhaps you don't start with 'Hello everybody' but with one sentence that pulls your audience straight into experiencing your story. Perhaps you show something, an object or slide that sets the tone for the rest of your fifteen minutes on stage. This is the huge difference between listening to and experiencing a story. It's up to you to decide what is most appropriate in your situation.

I believe that it's valuable and useful to take what you have learned from performances at TEDx conferences, whether it be your own or someone else's, with you in your daily professional life. I wouldn't encourage you to rewrite all your corporate presentations and TEDx-ify them into this intense experience that will blow your manager off his feet. You might just end up being Betty From Marketing, The Overly Creative One With Acting Aspirations. That wouldn't necessarily be a bad thing, but it depends on which branch you're in. Let's be fair: probably not every topic in every niche involves an "idea worth spreading."

You don't have to convert every situation into a compelling story. Many storytelling experts and storytelling consultants and campaign gurus will probably disagree with me on this, but I think one should be selective about which story is worth being mega creative with.

Using The Circle Method
You can use the Circle Method (get in, get out) while rehearsing your talk, to figure out which perspective works best for your message. Sometimes, a talk about a personal experience works best from your own perspective. But this doesn't mean that you can't switch perspectives during that talk, if this increases the possibility of your message landing with your audience the right way.

Let's dig a little deeper into this Circle Method and what it might do for you. Think of presenting your message as a circle you draw on the floor. You can step into the circle and present from the perspective of the message, yourself in a particular role, or another perspective. And you can step out of that circle at any given moment, to switch perspectives. This may sound somewhat cryptic, so I'll give you an example.

Let's say that you are to present a personal story of how you survived a nearly fatal bicycle accident and then spent six months in a rehabilitation center. You have rehearsed the entire talk from the perspective of the one who dealt with the situation in the story ("When I was nine years old, my parents bought me a bicycle"). You maintain this perspective throughout the talk ("and when I woke up in the hospital, I was so grateful that I was still alive, but I was facing a long time in the rehabilitation center."). Then you build up towards your key message, the takeaway for your audience ("So if you meet anyone that has been through a similar situation, please remember to always...").

Usually your talk would have three phases. Phase one: you introduce the topic. Phase two: You let the audience in on your fears and challenges. Phase three: you advise your audience to so something when they see someone who is going through a similar ordeal as you have just outlined. Your audience would probably admire your courage to share your story on stage, and would have a picture in their heads of you struggling and overcoming your hardship. The question is: would you have motivated them to change anything in their own lives? I think the structure and perspective can be optimized to enhance your result. This is when the Circle Method would be extremely useful.

Using the same bicycle accident example, the talk would be structured in another way. Phase one: "When I was nine years old, my parents bought me a bicycle." In phase two, you change perspective in such a way that the audience can relate to your parents: "I will never forget the look in my parents' eyes when I woke up in the hospital." Then, you step out of the circle of your own perspective and switch to enlightening statistics in phase three: "Every year, X bicycle accidents in our country leave X adults at the graves of their children. X children die every year." That's when the bomb drops. Your personal story then has meaning in another context: the context of your overarching message. This leads you to phase four: "Don't end up being one of these parents. Take care of [fill in your solution or idea]." And if you like, you can step back into your first perspective and share something about how you are today. This is a completely different effect, coming from the same source, which is your story and the need to raise the awareness of your audience.

You can get creative by choosing different perspectives. What if you look at this story from the perspective of someone who has accidentally hit a child with his car, and has suffered from intense guilt for the last thirty years? "I realize that this child would have celebrated her fortieth birthday. I can't even begin to imagine what her parents are feeling today." And then: "Don't end up being one of these parents. Take care of [fill in your idea]." Experiment with it while practicing your talk and discover which perspectives suit your message best.

The Circle Method can also enhance your corporate presentations. For instance, if you are working on building your brand, you should explore how you can illustrate your message in a story arc, and shift perspectives. Get creative.

Be mindful of your choice of words. They may change the world, but they might also be your last.

INTERVIEW

Caryn 't Hart de Wijkerslooth:
"If you want to speak at TEDx, you should already be living your idea today."

Caryn 't Hart de Wijkerslooth is Lecturer at Leiden University Medical Center and curator for TEDxDelft.

Tell me about your love for stories and storytelling.
Ever since I was a child, I've been an avid reader. I grew up in a Dutch family of storytellers, people who wanted to build up to the clou of stories in vivid conversations. It didn't come as a surprise that I decided to study Dutch Literature in college. The first moment I read stories in Mediaeval Dutch, I discovered and strongly felt: the person who wrote this, has had the same feelings that I do. It was like a hand reached out to me, out of those ancient scribblings. A handshake from the Middle Ages to the twenty-first century. Then I got even more curious. I discovered that many similarities bond the Middle Ages to today's society. I wrote my final thesis on how to describe unspeakable things in Mediaeval Dutch language.

The core of storytelling is to share stories based on our experiences, and to focus on what connects us to one another. The conclusion is that you are never alone. When you share your story, you are seen. And you can open your eyes to see other people by listening to their stories. It's just beautiful.

Where do you get your story fix?
Brilliant stories are everywhere. One of my favourite places to find compelling gems online is The Moth. (www.themoth.org). Many stories on The Moth are lovely, fascinating and pleasurable. I also find exceptional stories on RISK (www.risk-show.com)

by Kevin Allison. They are 'True Tales, Boldly Told', as his website promises. The stories are edgy, the podcasts often raw sketches of the North American social periphery.

What does any good story contain?
Wonderful stories are well researched, they have a turning point and plot twists, a protagonist and other important elements. But far more important than any nifty technicality or creative stunt, is the ability to captivate. A spellbinding story changes your world. Once I heard a man tell a story in such a compelling way, that by the end of his story, the whole room wanted to marry him, as a manner of speaking. Every wonderful story has a brilliant storyteller in itself, not just the other way around. Such a story reels you in. And what that element is, that alluring hook, is different for everyone.

You are speaker curator for TEDxDelft, you select stories. How do you find people with intriguing stories?
The way I stumble upon great stories for our TEDxDelft conference, is usually sheer magic. I'm always on the lookout for fascinating discoveries, and find gems everywhere. In bars, in schools, on the radio, in interviews. Trust me, good stories are everywhere to be found. My story antenna is active. And often people contact me, because they know I am a curator for TEDxDelft. The first thing I select my sources on is also the most important: it has to involve an idea worth spreading. If it is 'just' a story of personal resilience and overcoming hardship, it's not suitable for a TEDx conference. We're not a facility for therapeutical, cathartic sharing of experiences so someone may or may not feel better afterwards. It's always the quality that counts. That will always the biggest priority. If it's there, I jump on it. If it's not there, I let it go.

You have also trained speakers for their TEDxDelft performance. How do you usually like to start the preparation process with the speaker?
When I start the coaching process with one of our selected performers, I prefer to know as little as possible in advance. This

means that I avoid doing an internet search for this person. I want to be as open-minded and unprejudiced as humanly possible. During our first session, this person should be able to explain in a few sentences what the core idea worth spreading will be. If s/he can do that sufficiently, I have all the confidence I need to know that this will lead to a quality performance.

When do you know: this person has trained enough?
It's finding and recognizing the perfect balance. When we reach the point where the story path is captivating and the fluff has been deleted, it's a question of focusing on combining the speaker training with the core of someone's personality. If the sum of these elements work, we know the performance will probably go marvellously.

You never know whether or not someone has trained enough. But we can see when someone is over-trained. We usually detect that in time to do something about it. Our brains are built to process huge amounts of information long after we have taken in the information. The processing usually happens at night, when we sleep. Our brain filters superfluous stuff from the quality information without any additional effort. We wake up and usually things are more clear. The expression 'let me sleep on it' derives from that principle. When we suspect one of our coachees is over-trained, we advise him or her to stop practicing and leave the presentation copy and slides for the time being (up to fourteen days, if the time span allows that), and to pick it up a couple of days before the talk. That always helps improve the talk and to make it a more natural performance.

What should every speaker coach handle with their coachees?
The challenge is to connect the speaker with the best speaker coach for him or her. We always aim to make the best match. Our Head of Coaches takes that very seriously, and this is always a custom made match. We also try to take into account that some speaker coaches are like their coachees, sometimes introverts or extroverts. This is however not essential to the coaching process.

Sometimes speakers get two speaker coaches. We do not have a standard formula for that. Call it our gut feeling.

Every speaker coach works with the TEDx performer on crafting the perfect talk to bring across his or her message most effectively. They can eliminate parts of the draft talk quite ruthlessly, but all in the best interest of the final result. Stage performance, diction and 'carrying the story' are also very important elements we train speakers in.

What has been the most captivating moment, in relation to you and TEDx?
The moment that never ceases to amaze me, is when I'm in the audience or back stage, and I see what all of our preparation is leading to. To witness the result of all of our efforts.

What was the most nerve-racking moment thus far?
The most excruciating moment is the moment just before the story starts to captivate. You always hope this happens. There is always a nano second of intense fear. What if it won't happen? Fortunately, it almost always does happen. The release of that tension is enormous.

What have you learned since you've started being part of the TEDxDelft organization?
Working in this amazing TEDxDelft team has lead me to build even more trust and confidence in people, both in crew and speakers. It boils down to two essential questions. Can I help you? Can you please help me? These are two humbling yet extremely powerful questions, and it opens the gate to amazing conferences.

It's the learning journey and force of a story geek. Another thing I learned, was to take a break when I need one. I always take at least one day off after our TEDx events. Self care is a valuable necessity in times of intense effort and working together in this talented and powerful team.

Do you believe in templated performances, as in 'opening, build up tension, protagonist encounters hardship, rises above the occasion and shares his lesson with a big bang'?
I do and I don't believe in templated performances. They do not exist for nothing. Templates provide a framework to build on, and that makes it easier for us to make the story come into blossom. At the same time I don't believe in using templates too rigidly, if this means that the story doesn't get the liberty to bend the rules and distinguish itself from all other talks. Bending the rules can be refreshing, and if well done, it can blow you off your feet. Just make sure you bend the rules in a thought-out way and deliberately.

What are your tips for people who really want to speak at a TEDx conference or at other speaking engagements?
The most important thing should always be your idea. Make sure your idea isn't just about you. It has to be able to stand on its own. If it does and other people can benefit from it, give it a go. For the curators, the combination of the idea and the person sharing it is a good one. We can always make a better speaker. But we can't make a mediocre idea a good one with a magic wand.

If you want to increase your chances of being invited to a TEDx conference, you should already live and share your idea. You can't expect curators to notice you if you're not out there sharing your ideas.

Another suggestion for increasing your chances to get invited, is to just give us a call. Many people are afraid of being turned down. Although that fear is understandable, it isn't too helpful for getting ahead. If you truly think you have an idea that is a good match for a TEDx conference, contact us. And be prepared to be rejected or accepted. You'll just never know unless you try.
　The daily schedules of TEDx curators are often swamped with inspiring events where they might or might not meet new quality speakers. So take the liberty of inviting us. Woo us just a little bit.

"Stories can change the world, for better and for worse."

—Caryn 't Hart de Wijkerslooth,
curator TEDxDelft

What are your all-time favourite TED and TEDx talks?
One of our TEDx talks we are very proud of, is Boyan Slat's talk about cleaning the world oceans. His idea indeed was an idea worth spreading, and it is being carried out at the moment.

Another talk that inspired me, was Jamie Oliver's talk about improving young people's health and extending their life expectency by the simple yet far-reaching idea that anyone can learn how to cook healthy in just twenty-four hours. Ruby Wax's talk on dealing with depression ('What's So Funny About Mental Illness?') was also brilliant.

If you were on a TEDx stage, what would you share?
I really don't have to perform at a TEDx stage. My mission is what I am doing at this moment: finding the best stories and ideas worth spreading, and presenting them to the world through our speakers and conferences. Do you have any idea how awesome this job is? It's amazing!

What made you fall in love with the TED and TEDx concept?
It's simple, really. I have never discovered a single rule that didn't compute. It just all makes sense. On the one hand, TED and TEDx is very straightforward (ideas worth spreading), on the other hand, TEDx is emotional. TEDx has found me in 2012 through TEDxDelft founder Rob Speekenbrink, who is Europe's TEDx Ambassador since 2015. The first TEDx event in the Netherlands was in 2011, founded by Jim Stolze. We are very grateful to Jim and Rob.

Famous last words?
"Stories can change the world, for better and for worse."

"You have to accept your own mortality in order to able to live. If you take a role, take a risk.

That courage will open many parts of you. Don't be afraid to fall flat on your face."

—Hugh Jackman, *Inside the Actor's Studio*

WHAT A TEDx SPEAKER COACH TELLS YOU

The Last Supper

"You are welcome to visit us. Will you contact us to make an appointment?" The indescribable relief you can feel by reading a text message.

After a couple of days, I rang the doorbell, my heart pounding. "Hi! You're a day too early. But come in, it's okay." My foster mom prepared a lovely dinner and we shared a memorable evening. My foster dad didn't seem ill at all. I hadn't seen him for months, and I didn't have an visual image of him being ill. Things seemed eerily normal. It was as if my foster mom read my mind. "Yes, but it's true. It's an invisible predator." So it was.

The three of us shared a bottle of wine, and opened up another one. None of us were fierce drinkers, so the necessary courage was easily found. We had a lot to talk about, feelings to share and air to clear. It was pure quality time.

After a while, I said: "Look. I've been invited to speak at this event and I've been writing the speech since May. You two are the main characters in my talk. You have been since day one. I'm not supposed to discuss this because I have signed a non-disclosure agreement. But I'm breaking that contract now. Because we don't know whether or not you'll be with us to be there to hear it."
 "When is it?" Coen asked.
"In February," I said.
 "Sorry, I don't think ehm—", Coen replied.

Breaking the rules had never felt less rebellious.

"Coen, I promise you I will do my best. And everyone will hear what you two have done for me when I most needed it, all those years ago. I promise."

"I'll be there," Marianne said. I felt such a deep connection with her, right then and there. I still do.

"Have you been rehearsing?" she inquired.

"I have, and they have provided speaker coaches. They're very helpful."

"Yes, I know," Marianne replied, "one of my colleagues is a volunteer for TEDxDelft. They're well-organized, as far as I can tell from a distance. You'll be just fine. We know you can do this. Don't underestimate it, though."

"I won't," I replied, "And I'll get you — ehm...I'll get you a ticket."

KEY TAKEAWAYS

A Speaker Coach Is A Blessing

Having a speaker coach appointed to you by the TEDx organization is a blessing. These are people who know how to present a story. These are people who are trained to help you to perform better than you could've done without them. These are people who are willing and able to listen to your verbal piece and watch your concept presentation without prejudice. These are people who invest their valuable time in you because they believe you add something valuable to the equation of all speakers at the TEDx event.

Value for value. Not value for money.

Your speaker coaches are your safety zone. A safe haven where you can mess up a few times before getting it right. This however does not mean that they will appease your ego by saying that your talk is just about brilliant when in fact, there's still a lot to be done. The best speaker coaches create a safe environment in which you are able to receive harsh critique of your performance. And that's one of the key elements for you in crafting a story worth sharing: Being able to receive feedback and to digest it in the most mature way brings you where you want to be. A better speaker. A better storyteller. A better communicator. A better writer. A better performer. A better person.

Wait, what? A better person?

I strongly believe that you can indeed become a better person by being able to receive, digest and use useful feedback that you are given by people who have willingly and without hesitation invested in you and your story. When the source of feedback is a good one, you better listen and internalize. Sometimes it can take a few hours, even days, before you value the feedback you've just received. In those cases, I suggest that you hold off on replying directly after hearing the tough stuff. You might just have to get used to the insight. And yes, it may also be the case that the particular feedback you just got is something you plan on changing. In the end, it's your story that is on stage. And you are 'just' the messenger. If you truly love your story, you will do whatever it takes to make it the best you can. And getting over yourself is often a big part of this. You are not showing yourself off on stage. You are bringing the story to people. This is key.

Treat yourself and other people respectfully. And please, don't take yourself too seriously. Self reflection is very healthy.

Check the source, stay true to yourself
We all know examples of people who have vented harsh words under the guise of feedback, when in fact we already knew that these people didn't like us and/or our story one bit. It's impossible to make everybody happy. In case you run into people who are just a tiny bit too enthusiastic in venting their critique about you, look into their eyes. You'll see the value of their intentions. If you feel and see that these people have no positive association with your mission, let them go and release yourself from their feedback. You always have the liberty to do this.

INTERVIEW

Soness Stevens:

Always aim for: "There is none better in the world to share this message than you."

Soness Stevens is a Global Communications practitioner. She spoke at TED Worldwide and is a TEDx speaker twiceover. She's been called the #1 TEDx speaker coach in Asia, coaching over 100 TED & TEDx speakers around the world. As the Head Speaker Coach for multiple TEDx events, she makes sure speakers connect, engage and move audiences. She's also called The Professor at the univeristy where she teaches, authored two university textbooks on presentation skills, and published in a peer reviewed academic journal. You may have seen her weekly communications TV show on NHK or FOX TV. Soness is also the English voice for Hello Kitty. www.yourspeakingjourney.com

Soness, do you remember the first moment that you knew that speaking would be your way in life?
To me, speaking is not a way of life but an expression of love. Some people are striving to shine and perform. I've never been that way. By nature, I'm more of an introvert, or as the author Susan Caine would say, an omniver or ambivert. I prefer the quiet life, not a fan of small talk, but love to connect deeply. Go deep or go home!

   I was a global communications trainer at a major company in Japan. When I was a guest at a wedding party, a guy I met said I had a great voice for radio (obviously not the face for TV!). Turned out he's a celebrity, Pa-kun. He introduced me to his agent, and a few months later I had a nationwide broadcast English communications radio show. It paid pretty well for the hours and I was blissed out!

   Almost a year later, I quit my job to pursue voice full-time. But the week I quit my global communications day job, the radio program ended with no notice on the last day. Such is the talent industry in Japan. I was left jobless and incomeless. Fortunately I'd saved up about six months salary. I spent every day running along the beach visualizing my next steps. I could see a large stage—positive family communication! That's it!

Instead, three months later, a top university in Japan called because a friend who was teaching there needed a substitute for a semester. They asked if I could teach English. I apologized that I couldn't, but I'd be happy to teach presentation skills, in English. If you're two steps ahead, then you can teach it. I figured I was at least two steps ahead of shy students.

Still with this vision in my head, three months later, I auditioned with a few hundred other women for the voice of Hello Kitty. After weeks of endless VHS cassette study, and my neighbors through the paper thin walls in the next apartment wondering what I was doing, I landed the part of Hello Kitty. At the recording, I met Michelle who introduced me to this amazing company that produces events for audiences on 1,000+ nationwide for positive family communications.

Walking into the interview and audition, I heard them whisper to each other in Japanese, "Wow, what a nerdy girl!"

I wasn't the right look I didn't have the right training. I didn't have what they were looking for. They'd written me off in the first thirty seconds. Until they understood and saw: I don't care about the stage or speaking. It's all about connection. I can connect with the back row of an audience of a thousand just as easily as a conversation with one. Somehow, they saw this. I'm the first person they've ever hired on the spot. My vision became a reality.

I'm all about love and connection. In order to be an amazing speaker, it's not about how or what you speak, but the heart where it comes from. Love is compassion. Speaking is about compassion, not about 'just' teaching people new things. In my core, I know on a deep level that people also have experienced pain. We have the ability to become the mother that we need. To awaken that, is a beautiful and powerful thing.

You have been on three sides of the stage at TEDx: in the audience, on stage and backstage, coaching speakers. Where do you start when you start working with a speaker who is on the lineup to perform at a TEDx conference?
We always start with what is their intention on stage. I ask them why they're giving this particular talk and what they want to get out of it. I scan their overall intention. Then, I carefully listen to the core thesis parts of their talk. I get people to really focus on that.

I take coaching TEDx speakers very seriously and I invest a lot of time in helping them. Every speaker gets twenty hours of individual coaching before they're ready to perform on the TEDx stage. This has made me the number one sought after speaker coach in my Asia & Oceania. The amount of time and effort is also why speakers hire me after the event as well, for other events in their future. Often, we're building a long-term relationship. One of my events calls me 'The TEDx Whisperer." It makes me giggle.

At TEDx conferences, there is always a mix of introverts and extroverts in the lineup of speakers. Do you adjust your coaching strategies to them?
I like them to treat everyone the same way. Introverts want to be well prepared at all times, and know the power of dedication. Introverts immerse themselves deeply in their subject. Many introverts have to develop their skills in terms of focusing on connecting with their emotional life, and tapping into their emotions, and then deliberately using their emotions to engage with their audience. Engagement is key. I help introverts with this by offering a particular meditation assignment and an exercise for practicing connection. Making connection with your audience is also a physical sensation, even though it's happening in your head.

Extroverts are more into enjoying the moment, and often have to develop skills to remain focused on the exact contents of their talk. Many extroverts are so enthusiastic that they lose focus. I help them to channel their enthusiasm and to focus on their story.

"Have a beginner's heart. And always aim to envoke passion in other people."

—Soness Stevens

In an interview you once said: "you have to step up to lead the movement". Is this also one of the themes when you coach TEDx speakers?
I look at this more is in "There is none better in the world to share this message than you." Many people want to convince people to follow a movement.

Most speaker coaches will tell you to convince the audience of your idea. That's wrong. Here's why: the word 'convince'. 'Con' means 'with'. 'Vince' means 'conquer.' Who wants to be conquered? Certainly not me.

I say, our purpose is to enlighten, illuminate and persuade. The word 'persuade' comes from 'Per' meaning 'complete' and 'suade' or 'advise.' When we persuade, we are advising completely so the audience can get a new view.

I see TED & TEDx as a place to transform. Transform both the audience and you. That's why the TEDx talk you prepare with me will not only change the world, but change your life.

One of the things that I believe to be most powerful for speakers and performers, is to grow into the best version of who you can be. How do you feel about this?
Yes, absolutely. I've trained over a hundred TEDx speakers, coached over 20,000 people. And you know what, even I have a speaker coach. I always put together a team when I'm stretching my own comfort zone. Just keep developing yourself and your skills. Step up your game and by all means, get out of your own way!

At a TEDx conference, there are limits to the level of engagement one can have with the audience. Engagement however is important to let the message stick. How do you advise TEDx speakers about this?
This reminds me of improvisation comedy. Comedians have to create a scene from nothing. This means that you can create whatever you want. It's a scene without rules. But when you

add a few rules and boundaries, this triggers you to be more creative. This is a good thing. So boundaries and restrictions are good things. We as human beings are problem solving creatures. Limitations are good. So find a way to connect to the audience in a way that suits you.

In one of your Show-n-Tell video's, you share a powerful phrase: 'Nourish your process with feedback'. For most of us, learning how to receive feedback is a process is itself. And when rehearsing for something like a TEDx talk, the stakes are also a bit higher than rehearsing for a five minute financial quarterly presentation. When a TEDx speaker-to-be shows his or her progress to a speaker coach, receiving feedback can be somewhat intimidating for them. Do you adjust your feedback style for different kinds of coachees? Of course I adjust my coaching technique to the person who is presenting in front of me. Coaching is also people reading. As a university professor, I'm dealing with different kinds of people. When you're dealing with students with zero background, or the boss, or other professors, or CEO's, there is a bit of diference between personalities and levels of expertise. As a business pro, you have to be able to read people. You have to be interested in people and understand where they are coming from. And more importantly: what they want to achieve.

I listen to that particular person, and then by understanding their motivations, key language and reactions, I can decide what kind of feedback is approporate. You can't tiptoe around as a speaker coach; you always go for the best quality possible. In the relationship between a speaker coach and the coachee, there must be a level of understanding of openness and honesty. I always ask in the beginning where someone wants to go. I look for ways to contribute to their best achievement possible.

Soness, you are from the United States originally. You have been living in Japan for 20 years now. Have you noticed any cultural differences in speaking coaching practice between the United States and Japan?

My first priority is to take the coachee to his or her next level of expertise. I can't say that the differences between Japan and the US are absolute; this depends on the person and the speaker that I'm coaching. I am based in Japan, and about thirty percent of my coachees are foreigners. These people are very culturally aware. Japanese people are beautifully receptive and they will implement feedback fully. They recognize when the feedback connects with them. They have great dedication.

My Your Speaking Journey clients tend to be global citizens, many from Europe, Australia, New Zealand, Asia, and North America.

When you give feedback to the speaking performances of Americans, you can be a little more direct. In terms of cultural differences. I also discovered that Australians and Europeans have a similar, though not quite as shy, humility about speaking like Japanese.

My coachees in Japan have 'a beginner's heart'. I just love that about them. They will trust your guidance and integrate the learnings that they receive. European and Oceanians will rather say "I need support", which is equally interesting and valuable.

I advise every speaker to find out how the expected demographic is in the audience, before the event takes place. Ask the organizer what he wants and needs specifically, so you can be at service as best as possible. Every event has its own atmosphere and purpose.

Have a beginner's heart. Hold compassion for your who you are speaking, not to, but with. Always keep your highest intention as love.

The best talks in the world are not about the ones who gave them.

SPEAKER STYLE: CONNECTING WITH YOUR AUDIENCE

A Part Of Them, A Part Of Me

In challenging times, inspiring words can be soothing. I stumbled upon one of Les Brown's inspirational quotes that resonated with me: "Things may happen around you, things may happen to you, but the only things that really count are the things that happen in you."

Like my father, I had been a natural speaker since the moment I started speaking in my business. But sometimes, things happen that are too big for words.

After returning from a short business trip to Ireland, my foster mom sent me a text message, telling me that I'd have to visit in the following days, because that would probably be the last opportunity to speak to her husband.

The last time I saw my foster dad, I held his hand for over an hour. I didn't have words that could ease his discomfort. Nothing I'd say could change any of it. Lost for words.

The next day, Coen passed away.

The day after, recording the promotional videos for TEDxDelft was scheduled. A studio had been booked, so I had to find a way to postpone my outpouring of grief. I woke up with puffy eyes from having cried and with a built up fatigue. I splashed cold water on my face and just took it one minute at a time. I don't exactly know how I did it, but I managed to stay focused after hardly having slept. While driving to the recording studio, I tried my best not to think of anything at all. It took us about half an hour to come up with one minute of copy for the promotional video for my talk and to record it.

Afterwards, I went to my foster parents' home, to help with all of the arrangements that had to be made. A bizarre contrast with what I was doing one hour earlier. I cancelled my business appointments for the next days and took my time to deal with this. And I had to come up with words for Coen's service.

The evening before the service, I went to sleep wishing the words would pop up the next morning. They did. A few sentences on a small piece of paper, just to have something to hold on to, like a buoy in swirling water. At my parents' funerals, I hadn't spoken. Nobody had expected me to say anything back then, and I couldn't think of anything to say. I was fourteen years old at the time, and quite frankly, the whole thing had been intimidating.

But now, all I wanted to do was to do something useful and to give something, even if they were just words. In my work as a speaker, I always feel part of the audience, and that they are a part of me. But I had never experienced this connection and emotion on such a visceral level as I did during that service. It was the shortest and most difficult speech I had ever given. What helped me most at that moment was imagining Coen telling me: "Just do it."

Where it appeared to be quite the challenge to strip the TEDx talk of unnecessary things and words, it was the opposite when I wrote the words for Coen's service. I only said what I could manage before choking up, and nothing more than the words that could honour him at that vulnerable moment. I was finding the balance between how I was feeling and what I had to do.

One hour later, a trumpeter played The Last Post, the bugle call that is sounded at military funerals to indicate that a soldier has gone to his final rest.

KEY TAKEAWAYS

Keep Your Audience Close

'Ubuntu' is an idea present in African spirituality that means "I am because we are". It is a beautiful principle of connection, community and caring. In the practice of speaking, to me this is about feeling a part of the whole room, and the audience being a part of me. And then I'm trying to be the vehicle of the story, balancing between leaving my ego at the door and leveraging my strengths.

In most of my presentations in business settings, there is room for improvisation and lots of interaction with the audience. This is something I value dearly. Truly connecting.

The Big Question: Do You Think It Is About You?
At a TEDx conference, your message is not about you. Your performance is not about you. I profoundly believe this to be true. It is about your message, the purpose of this message and how you bring it to your audience accordingly. You shape this message in the best possible way, with all necessary skills. As much as your story may speak for itself, it still has to be performed professionally. You are (or can learn how to be) the master of your skills set. And you can grow into the best version of YOU possible.

Once a speaker feels the humility that a TEDx rehearsing phase requires, he/she knows: it isn't about me. And it shouldn't. Because if it were about me, the message wouldn't be the center of attention. I may be the medium for this message. I may be in the centre of the stage. But this doesn't make me the message.

Communication and media professionals might think of Marshall McLuhan's 1960's statement 'The medium is the message'. In the light of performing at a TEDx conference, I agree up to a point.

The one who brings the message has to perform well in order to get his/her message across. If you fail to do so, your message fades into oblivion. So far, I agree with McLuhan. But if a speaker would stop there and focus merely on performing well, an essential facet would be lost: the effect of the message. When a speaker performs brilliantly, there is always the risk of being perceived as 'a brilliant speaker'. Which is, ofcourse, rather wonderful. But when that is all that remains of the talk, I think a big opportunity is lost. The opportunity to change the world. Sounds big, right? 'To change the world'. I think it can be done. I did it in my own way. And you can do it, too. I think everybody who speaks at TED, TEDx, weddings, funerals, birthdays, board rooms, book presentations and on any other occasion, and manages to let the talk not be about them or about their performance, is changing the world. Because you are transferring the message to other people in a way that it doesn't have to stick 'just' to you.

The best talks in the world are not about the ones who gave it.

"I have a dream", Rev. Martin Luther King said. This talk wasn't about Martin Luther King. It was about the dream he had. Not just his dream, but a dream he wanted to plant in the minds of everyone who listened. It was every listener's dream, the one of hope. This wish, this image, resonates in minds even today.

"Ich bin ein Berliner", Pres. John F. Kennedy said, when he visited Berlin. This talk wasn't about Kennedy being German or an avid Berlin lover. It wasn't about Kennedy at all. It was about connection. This talk directly tapped into the audience's yearning to be included, to be loved, to be connected.

Before you even heard these speakers say these words, they have felt the lesson the words represented. That's why they are able to let their talk stick with you.

The best talks in the world are about the ones who listened to and felt every single word in them in the most personal way possible.

Martin's and John's speeches have this in common. They connected brilliantly with the audience by not being a talk about themselves but instead about the ones who were listening. There a lot of great speakers who don't even think about getting over themselves, because the thought that their message was about them was never in their minds. They are capable of bringing their message because it is their nature to share and to remain curious for the rest of their lives.

Getting Over Yourself Leads You To That Sacred Place
When you decide to truly connect to your audience, to bring your message the best way you can, and once you accept the concept of the message (regardless which message it may be) not being about you, you can open the door to a sacred place.

And the best way to get your audience to listen to your talk is to tap into their world, their minds, their fears, their wishes. And that is a very sacred place to be. Consider it an honour to be let into their minds, their world, their fears, their wishes. You are a guest. Behave accordingly. And once you're there, make a valuable connection. It doesn't have to be a one hundred percent pleasant connection. It may be confrontational. It may be scary. It may be daunting. It may be hilarious. It may be emotional. All of this is perfect...as long as you're truly connected and in the moment, without your ego disturbing your audience's attention. Be real. Get over yourself. And connect wholehearted.

Get To Know Your Audience
Knowing who you will be speaking to is of vital importance. Not knowing what kind of people will be in your room can either make or break your credibility. I can't even count the times I have been in an audience with a speaker pouring out insane amounts of statistics and facts, trying to impress everyone in the room. Often, the audience consists of people who are either well-informed or not too familiar with the presented topic. In both cases, pouring out statistics without placing them in context for the target group is usually counter-productive, because well-informed people hear

The best way to get your audience to listen to your talk is to tap into their world, their minds, their fears, their wishes. And that is a sacred place to be.

information they already knew. For newbies, statistics don't ring a bell because they're not familiar with the content. So while the speaker is giving his best, everything he's got, the audience remains disconnected to his message. It also often happens that a speaker doesn't put in the effort to customize at least a small part of the information in his presentation, so that the audience can relate to it. A simple way to avoid this horror is to do some research before a presentation, dig into issues that the target group isstruggling with and then provide a solution. Additional backgroundinformation and statistics can also be useful, but shouldn't be used as a means to reel your fresh audience in.

Relating To Them
The way people can relate to your talk depends on the nature, topic and level of customization of your presentation. If you will be speaking at a TEDx conference, you can't focus on a specific target group or niche other than 'TEDx attendees with a broad interest in topics in technology, entertainment and design', which covers just about anything for anybody. But if you will be giving your signature speech at a business club for female entrepreneurs in the lifestyle branch, for instance, you can tweak elements to fit your audience. Will you be speaking in front of 2,000 people who are also public speakers? In that case, a whole other dynamic switches on. You'll have to not only enrich your audience with useful information, but also wow your colleagues with your performance.

This can be a rather daunting experience for any speaker, because many people in your audience might wish that they were standing on the very stage you currently occupy, and they will judge you perhaps a tad more hashly than they would someone who they don't consider a colleague. The stress level will peak to extra-terrestrial level in the event your speech will be on the topic of speaking. The preparation time for performances such as these will probably be longer than other presentations.

The Liberating Thing About Losing Power
Perhaps you are afraid to lose your power. Perhaps you fear being caught up with people supposedly smarter than you. Perhaps you

feel you're not getting the public confirmation you intrinsically need. I have learned the hard way, at several moments in my life, that fear was holding me back. Fear, envy and negative power are deceiving messengers. They cover up that you're not capable of fulfilling your own needs and ambitions. There is a positive side to this: having these emotions indicate that there is a lesson to be learned. When you're capable of fulfilling your needs, wishes and ambitions, you're not worrying about power anymore. You'll be free and capable.

Perhaps this is what Yoda meant when he said "Train yourself to let go of everything you fear to lose." (in Star Wars, 'The Empire Strikes Back'). Do as Yoda said.

Positive Power vs. Ego
Your audience gets to be in a sacred place as well. For a moment, they get to enter your world, your thoughts, your emotions and your vocabulary. As much as you have to be a good host to them, they have to be courteous guests at your place. And a room where someone is pouring out their thoroughly rehearsed words, and where people are taking them in, is sacred. TEDx is such a place.

In that sacred place there is no need for battling egos. There's no need for wanting to be right all the time. There's no need for having to please everyone in the room. There's no need for clenched teeth and grit.

It is a place of equality, connection, wanting to learn and planting seeds for your message to find the rest of the world. Being in that place is refreshingly liberating. Your message will do its job if you present it in a way that suits the message.

From this liberated state, it's so much easier to let yourself be seen, and to use all of your abilities, talents and positive power to excel in presenting. You may and should use all these powerful tools to bring your message. It's essential that you use these qualities. You don't have to claim power. You don't have to show that you are the smartest or most talented person in the room or anything else. You don't have to talk about these things either. It's utterly unnecessary.

Use your power in your performance to the advantage of the message. That way, these talents, abilities and positive power shine back at you. And your audience will perceive you accordingly. It's a force of nature. You get back whatever you beam out.

When your audience doesn't respond to your topic
If you perform in front of a business club, and you share a personal story about a life-changing event in your youth, there's always the risk of people not feeling comfortable showing their emotions. There's always the risk of having a mis-match with your topic in relation to your audience: they might just not be into it. You can't make everybody happy. And you don't have to.

Every once in a while, you might encounter one person in the audience who is showing passive-aggressive behaviour. Not responding to questions. Looking the other way. Avoiding eye contact. When asked a question, just answering in single word sentences. Whatever your thoughts and emotions are about this: remain calm and courteous. Stay in a zone of curiosity and try to connect. If this doesn't work, then refocus on the complete audience. They deserve the best of you!

This usually does not happen at TEDx conferences, because everyone in the room is already open to hearing stories about all kinds of topics. But in other contexts, people may not always be open to new experiences or stories that stretch their perspectives. This does not necessarily mean that your message hasn't landed. It just means that your performance may feel somewhat lonesome to you. It has happened to me as well. I was invited to speak about my experiences growing up without my parents. When you talk about the topic of death, many people get this look in their eyes of a bunny on a highway. By hearing your vulnerable story of being an orphan, many people feel confronted with their own fear of mortality. That's understandable. It's not a bad thing if you want to break taboos and discuss sensitive topics freely. But you do have to take responsibility for guiding your audience back to their safety zone.

"The X-Factor exists by the grace of communication. It has to be given to you by the person with whom you are communicating."

—Henkjan Smits,
talent coach Business X-Factor,
radio presenter, former coach TEDxAmsterdam

The X-Factor

The X-Factor is a music talent competition television franchise created by Simon Cowell. It originated in the United Kingdom. In the Netherlands, the go-to expert on X-factor is talent coach Business X-Factor, radio presenter and former TEDxAmsterdam coach and Henkjan Smits. To understand the essence of the phenomenon X-factor, I have asked him for his insights on this. Henkjan shares valuable tips.

"The X-Factor exists by the grace of communication. You can't get it by yourself; It has to be given to you by the person with whom you are communicating. It's essential to get the X-Factor from your audience.

You can't get the X-Factor with just a few tips and tricks. But there are a few essential points for public speakers who want improve their performance.

- ☐ Establish an authentic connection with your audience.
- ☐ Make sure that you are an authority on your topic.
- ☐ If you don't know everything about your topic, admit it, don't beat around the bush.
- ☐ Do not worry about what others think of you.
- ☐ Do not be afraid of a blackout, but show your vulnerability.
- ☐ make your audience aware of the takeaway ('What's in it for me').
- ☐ Stand still, don't pace back and forth on stage.
- ☐ Ask rhetorical questions to keep the attention.

And as Michael Jackson already stated: "The three most important things are rehearsing, rehearsing and rehearsing"."

"You have to love yourself. Only if you love yourself and dare to show yourself, you are able to move your audience."

—Edo van Santen, Pitch Coach
www.edovansanten.com

INTERVIEW

Lianne Ebbinkhuijsen:

"There is nothing more vulnerable, naked and truth-telling than speaking."

Lianne Ebbinkhuijsen is an international public speaker, specialising in teaching professionals how to speak to sell their idea without losing themselves in the process.

How would you describe your own speaker style?
My preferred style is a teaching style, but over the years I have learned to be more flexible in my style so that I can switch from my introvert nature into my extraversion. What also has helped me a lot is having learned to evenly balance my attention while speaking. To me, it's important to have a placid basis, from where I can step into my leading role and then to go back again. My intention is always to be present with the audience and with myself at the same time. From there I can come up with what I had prepared in the first place.

When did you know you were going to be a professional speaker?
When I was a child, I was always in awe of the Eurovision Song Contest. The performances, the tension, the joy, it was a special package. Then the first seed was planted. However, my pivotal public speaking moment occurred when I was working in the corporate arena as a young certified public accountant. Back then, I worked in cultures with lots of integrity issues and hidden agendas so I felt unsafe to show my real self.

One day I had to do an important presentation in front of an international committee of twenty-two men, before which I had made a fool of myself two years before. So on that particular day I was very nervous, not knowing how my speech would go. And it was there and then, I decided to stop what I had been doing for years; I decided to stop sustaining an image of a strong and professional woman, I decided not to listen to the conflicting voices in my head and..surrendered. So when it was my turn to present, I decided to just stand up, get in front of the boardroom and allow myself this uncertainty of what would happen. I stood up there for a moment, looked in their eyes and I had my best speech ever, resulting in a one hundred percent buy-in for a new and risky idea! And since this 'defining moment' of letting my walls down and not working so hard for safety, I just wanted more! For the first time in my life it was easy for me to influence others in an authentic and highly effective way. Finally I proved to myself that it can be easy, as deep down I have this belief that there is always an easy way to get where you want to go. That is why I became passionate about speaking, sales and influence.

What made you decide on your speaking topic?
Choosing which topics I would speak about only became relevant when I became an entrepreneur; the moment when it became necessary to sell myself. I started reflecting on what had happened, that day in the boardroom, that ultimately had lead to my decision to quit my job and started studying themes like influence, business, sales, impact and speaking. I learned that one of the most important keys to success is to learn how to sell yourself and your ideas to people without losing yourself.

How would you describe the X-factor in public speaking?
For the X-factor in you to come out it's vital to be yourself on stage. We hear that a lot of course but it goes way beyond the mantra "Just be yourself, and you'll be fine!" Where I see the X-factor in others is when they are fully present; the being portion of speaking. And when I explored the concept of 'presence' for myself I boiled the sweet spot of when it's there down to three points; that moment where I can feel (1) myself IN the (2) room WITH (3) the audience. This is crucial in my opinion. So you have to be aware of all three at the same time. I like to see 'presence' in terms of relational presence; being with other people, your audience. So then the question comes up 'what can I do to be present?'

The X-factor in action is seeing someone who perhaps may be nervous or anxious even, but who does not solve this discomfort by behaving as such. I always say 'there is nothing wrong with feeling fear. However, it harms your persuasion power when you 'do fear'. Doing fear can look like talking too fast, smiling a lot, moving too much, arrogance, making yourself small, leaning into a slide deck and so on. So instead of talking too fast or smiling a lot etcetera you do nothing. You don't give yourself instructions to release or let go, just do nothing. Even if it's just for a few seconds.

It's natural and normal to feel some adrenaline, especially at the start of your talk. So see that as a normal part of the process rather than to fight it. It's better to just notice that your veins are full of adrenaline than trying to solve it. You lose the X-factor when you 'do' nervous.

Perhaps you already know that you sometimes do these things. Perhaps you don't. Either way, your audience picks up on these signals. They can smell them, as a matter of speaking. Just like you recognize those signs when you see someone battling their nerves on stage. It couldn't hurt if you record one or two of your presentations or record a rehearsal for one of your upcoming presentations. Watch yourself and you will discover how you 'solve' discomfort and uncertainty.

A first step to get to this 'relational presence' where your X-factor resides, is being available with relaxed eyes with one person in your audience at a time. Try to relax your eye sockets first. Look at a picture on the wall or through a window and you can feel your eyes relax. That is the first step. It always works.

Charismatic people, like President Barack Obama for instance, often have very few 'solutions' for any discomfort or uncertainty when they are in the spotlight. You can somehow feel that they are comfortable, no matter what.

Do you use specific tools to engage with your audience?
To set up the first connection with the audience after setting my intentions, is to use an ice-breaker. This of course depends on the size of the audience. If it's a large room, I usually ask people to raise hands after I asked them a question. If it's a small room,

"Story and message have to be evenly balanced in your performance. In the end, your message has to stick. But to make that happen, you have to use the power of story."

—Lianne Ebbinkhuijsen

I ask one or two open ended questions and interact with individual people and then direct it back to my topic. Inclusion is very important; making sure that the whole audience can feel they are in the right place. They have to be part of my story as much as I have to be part of their experience. I also love giving the audience an exercise to share something with someone sitting next to them. That way, the presentation is a shared experience and it gets them all in.

What is more important, story or message?
Story and message have to be evenly balanced in your performance. In the end, your message has to stick. But to make that happen, you have to use the power of story. Your goal should be to change something in their world. To get your audience to want to change, you have to connect to them on an emotional and intellectual level.

Paint a mental picture of what you are trying to sell. Whether it's a message or a product. A mental picture is something your audience can see in their mind's eye. And the best mental pictures to give them are the ones where they can see or picture themselves using your idea or concept.

Is there something you do not wish to ever see again in the performance of any speaker?
An enormous turnoff for me is when someone starts laughing at his own jokes. I can't believe how many people still do this. Laughter can be contagious, but not if you're the first one laughing about something you just said. I wish people would stop doing that.

Another pet peeve: when someone appears on stage with an excuse. Excuses are always unnecessary. Regardless what they're about. Some people start with an excuse about their clothing, that they miss a glossy slide deck, their lack of preparation time or exhausted state because of flight delay. If you are present with me, it doesn't matter. Just bring your story and connect! Making excuses just gets your audience off track.

Would you share one or two of the most valuable lessons you have learned in your career as a speaker?
A juicy lesson I once learned, is how to deal with a heckler in the room. Perhaps you have been in a room where one person is practically unpleasable, and starts commenting negatively on anything the speaker is trying to share. Someone who is criticizing just for the sake of it. One of the most powerful things you can do, regardless of what anyone else says or does, is to let go of the need to be right. That is really the first step and often the first step is in our minds. For instance: someone in your audience, let's call him Mr. Heckler, completely disagrees with you on a crucial statement you have just presented with everything you've got. He says something like "That's bogus! You're wrong! It's not A, it's B!" You might consider saying like "Okay, I hear you. You say B instead of A. Is there anyone else in the room that feels this way? Please show hands." This is powerful, because you bring the resistance to the surface. This way, the tension can't get to a boiling point.

Another advantage of this method is that you show your respect for the audience. You want to keep them close. If there are people who agree with Mr. Heckler, you will know who they are, and you can reply by saying: "Okay, that's cool. You can have a different point of view on this. However, I believe in (fill in facts one, two and three), and I have experienced that this can lead to (results)." You reel them back in like that. I try to stay open to sentiments in the room. It's the only thing I can do. And let's not forget that I'm still the speaker in that situation. I have to show my leadership skills when necessary. This is typically a situation where leadership is required. We're in this together.

Another lesson is a simple one. And as simple as it may sound, it's not easy, but please keep the time! For me this was one of the most difficult things to learn and I still see many inexperienced speakers miss out here. Develop a sense of speaking time and keep the time. The tension that you build up in your talk will drop if you don't. It's also a way to show respect to your audience and they will respect you back for it.

Who inspires you?
Cathrine Sadolin from Denmark has made quite the impression on me. Cathrine is a woman who suffered from asthma, but at the same time, she aspired to become an opera singer. She believed it was possible, so she developed what she needed to make it happen: a complete vocal technique. And she succeeded. She shares her experiences, and inspires many people by speaking about this journey, by singing and teaching others how it's done. Many people benefit from her insights and experiences. Some of Cathrine Sadolin's talks can be watched online. Oprah Winfrey is another great inspiration. For many reasons, she is a role model. As a performer, as a business woman and as a human being. Dutch performer Karin Bloemen is a singer and comedian with unlimited creativity. She makes me believe there's always a new idea. Karin lives her talk.

Are there still things you would like to learn or experience as a professional speaker? Do you still have dreams or not yet fulfilled ambitions?
Dreams and ambitions are very important to me. If you don't have these, you wouldn't recognize them when they tapped you on the shoulder. I would just love to create a theatre piece. And I would love to help more of my dream clients: people who have created life-changing products. Help them find ways to spread their idea in a big way. I want to contribute to their life-changing launch. I'm always working on ways to grow my own business. It's a wonderful journey. Writing books and a TEDx talk are also on my mood board. The biggest dream I have though is for my three children to grow up as happy, infinite beings.

Famous last words?
Besides singing there is nothing more vulnerable, naked and truth telling than speaking. It requires full discovery of yourself. You cannot hide, evade or escape when you are on stage. It is a process, it requires dedication. Speaking for me is the number one tool to get to that stage of being a mature entrepreneur quickly. That type of freedom is something everyone deserves to enjoy. So speak!

Take a creative approach
to learning new ways
to improving yourself.
Be open to a humbling
yet wonderful experience.

REHEARSING YOUR TALK

Walk The Talk

It was a generous gesture of the TEDxDelft organization to provide their speakers with coaches. It's a very wise decision to make use of this facility, even—and perhaps it's better to say especially—for experienced speakers. Many performers at TEDx conferences are seasoned speakers. Professors who have given lectures for decades. Entrepreneurs and researchers who have defended their ideas hundreds of times. And consultants and other speakers who have built a body of work. It's easy to fall into the trap of feeling too confident because of this, while the wise choice would be to embrace this fresh new lesson of learning how to perform in a way you are not accustomed to.

Adjusting the way you speak is one thing, but combining this with learning a written speech of approximately two thousand five hundred words is another. To me, it felt like being a speed skater on ice, being asked to try figure skating and to rehearse for the Olympic finals in a couple of weeks—all at the same time. You may be talented and experienced, but in another area than what you're being asked to do.

I shared my concern with Wieneke, one of my friends. She suggested that I call a mutual friend that I'd lost contact with. I instantly felt that this was good advice, for our mutual friend, Ric, had been acting and directing in theatres for years. He and I were very much alike in terms of whirling creativity and enthusiasm. I knew that I had to learn something I hadn't done before: learning a long piece by heart and perform it in a relaxed but determined fashion.

Ric answered the phone. "Whoa. It's a mighty long time ago since we talked, Jo. Good to hear your voice". The feeling was mutual.

After we exchanged pleasantries, I cut to the chase and said: "Ric, I need help preparing for something, and you're the only person in the world I know that can help me get where I need to be. And I trust you completely. Will you help me?"

Despite the fact that Ric and I hadn't been close for years he was very forthcoming, and we scheduled a meeting to go through my material. That in itself was already a precious gift. We met at my office, and I read the draft of my speech. Ric listened carefully, and offered many suggestions for making it more concise. Which was very necessary by the way, because at that stage it still took over thirty-two minutes to say what I ultimately had to perform in a maximum of eighteen minutes. We chopped relentlessly and started rehearsing.

First, I was reading out loud in front of him. I felt very nervous, but Ric was understanding. Fortunately, Ric is one of the very few people who can laugh at me, while slapping his knees, for messing things up. It's just one of those things that indicate that there is a great deal of trust.

Being able to let someone laugh at you, and laughing with them about your own mistakes. The first meeting was a success. And we knew that another one would be very necessary.

The Cards

Ric gave me one of the most useful assignments ever. Honestly, I still use this technique today, for many occasions. He told me to make stepping stones in my story and to write them as single words on cards. First, I started with over twenty-five cards, each with a key word on them. We laid the cards out on the stage floor in chronological order, and I walked slowly past the cards, while telling the story in short sentences.

The next step was speeding up the process of telling the story. A faster pace. And again. And again.

"Ric, I keep skipping one or two vital elements when I'm telling the story faster and faster."

"Go on."

Our second meeting was in the theatre where Ric is a director.

We used the stage to help me get accustomed to different styles of 'filling the stage' and to find a way to connect with the audience, even when there is little room to do so.

We laid out the timeline of ten cards on the stage floor. Ric directed. "Okay, make your entrance." I wasn't used to making an entrance, because usually I had already been in the rooms I had presented in. It took a bit of getting used to, but after a few minutes, things went well.

"Okay, let's follow the paper trail and reconstruct the story like we did the last time." I obliged. "Uhm, okay, so this is still twenty-seven minutes. We have to cut some meat out of this. Let's do this now." We did. And in high speed tempo. With certain sentences, Ric said: "Yeah, great sentence, but you wrote it for you, and not for the audience. Skip this." Step by step, the story core became clearer, and I kept working on improving. At one point we knew: this is the perfect amount.

Ric suggested that I remove ten cards from the pile of keyword cards, so that we'd be left with fifteen cards, and then try to tell the storyline in the same fast-paced way. I needed some nudges in the right direction, but it worked. The next step was to reduce the pile of cards to ten. These ten cards became the frame for the whole TEDx talk. I still have the cards. The key phrases on them are: Valentine's Card, No Safety Net, Cabinet, Myths, Philanthropism, Coen, Grim Reaper, Judgment, Ally, Notice/Facilitate/Empower. Once I internalized these ten stepping stones, I knew nothing could go wrong in terms of holding the story line.

"Right, so now I have to learn it by heart."
"Yup."
"Suggestions?"
"Download the Line Learner app from the AppStore. I use this all the time to internalize roles in our plays. Record your voice while reading the piece out loud. First in one go, and then in ten pieces, matching your stepping stone cards. Live with your lines for a while. If I can do this, you can."

This was solid advice. It worked like a charm. After a few weeks, I had to perform my piece for the speaker coaches. They glanced at each other after I finished, and concluded that I was overtrained. I knew the piece by heart, but it felt forced. This was a comment I had never gotten in over ten years. If I knew one thing, it was that I never spoke in a forced way. And that was exactly the key in this: I had never had to learn a long piece by heart. I had always spoken in a natural way, using a few key words as a guideline during performances. This was just a completely different approach, which lead me to new challenges. Like performing in a forced way. I took the team's advice and let it rest for a while. This helped a great deal.

The wonderful thing about the human brain is that it continues to work while you're letting things go for a while. Rest is very important for internalizing information in your long-term memory.

After ten days, I listened to my recording in the Line Learner app once more, to check whether or not I still felt the whole piece. I did. I never touched it again. After rehearsing with Ric, I decided to show my progress to my friends Dick and Mary. I knew them for years already, and I wanted a fresh take on my talk, the contents of it, the performance and anything that popped up. This was useful and made me feel more confident.

I still use the cards to rehearse performances. Not just that, I also rebuilt my company, my home and other projects with the cards method. It helps me prioritize my thoughts and it lets me discover even greater ambitions in creative projects. This is working brilliantly for me. Thank you, Ric!

KEY TAKEAWAYS

The Learning Puzzle

You've established what you want to share in your talk. You have written a script (perhaps even though you weren't used to doing this). You feel every word when you're reading your script. And now, you have to learn your talk by heart.

Learn the whole thing by heart. Every single word. All of it. For me, it meant that I had to unlearn what I had learned.

If you're at all like me, you haven't memorized large amounts of text since high school, when we had to recite poems and learn rows of irregular verbs. For me, high school is 22 years ago. My grey matter can do amazing things without immense effort, but learning excessive amounts of copy is not one of them.

That's what I thought. I thought wrong.
Even if you haven't learned anything by heart in a gazillion years, it can be done. You might consider trying the card method I used with Ric.

Carry the cards with you in your bag. Do not just take pictures of them with your smartphone. Actually carry the physical cards with you, and leaf through them at any moment you feel the least bit insecure about your performance. The tactile experience while practicing will help you memorize your speech much faster. You internalize it more easily when your body is connected to it. Actors know this, and use this information to their advantage.

Please don't make the mistake of only rehearsing in your mind. Let your talk sink into your body. Remember, it's not just your mind that has to bring this talk to the stage. Performing is a strongly intertwined body and mind task. Treat it as such.

Fast, faster, warp speed

Another way to internalize your story arc is to tell the whole thing in no more than two minutes. In Dutch, we call this method an 'Italiaantje'. You can compare this to the 'quick pitches' in the film industry: film producers explain the entire film they want to make in just two sentences. Practicing with this technique might improve your memory skills. A handy tip is to combine this quick pitch method with thinking of pictures with the keyword cards. An image can say more than a thousand words, they say.

Reading your script as a bedtime story might not seem like the most relaxed way to learn, but it certainly helps. Read the script once and go to sleep. At moments when you don't feel stress, your brain works even harder for you. Science is backing this one up: during sleep (also those luxurious short daytime naps!) your brain helps you to memorize your lines. Really!

If you don't want to read out loud to your friends or partner, you might also consider reading to your pet. I read the whole ruddy thing to my red furry cat. He might not have been too impressed, but it helped.

Something I also found very helpful was to record rehearsals, including the ones that were not on a stage. I used the video camera and a tripod, the setup I use for creating e-learning videos for my students and clients. You might also use your smartphone. The camera features in smartphones are getting better every day.

Yes, it takes a bit of getting used to seeing yourself on video, if you haven't experienced this before. But stay with it: you will become more comfortable and results will improve rather quickly.

During the phase of rehearsing, I was asked to speak at a university about child grief and our WesternOrphans.org project. I covertly rehearsed the techniques that Ric had taught me. This gave me the reassurance that the method worked.

Accept that this will take more rehearsing time than you might have expected. I hear this also from many other TEDx speakers, with all levels of experience. Did you know Steve Jobs rehearsed his talks weeks in advance? You truly have no excuse not to rehearse. And yes, the easier it looks on stage, the harder preparing for it was.

If you have been invited to speak at a TEDx conference but you feel you have not been given enough time to write and rehearse, have the guts to call it off. This may sound strange, because speaking at an event like that may have been on your bucket list for some time. But trust me when I say that some people have performed, and still get a knot in their stomach, when they remember the experience of standing there, not well enough prepared. This is not always the speaker's fault; sometimes it's the curator's enthusiasm and spontaneity that triggers them to invite a particular speaker.

Don't get me wrong: I don't think those speakers shouldn't have been invited to perform. But I do think that it would have been more fair to the speaker, the organization and the audience, to postpone that speaker's performance (perhaps until the next event of that TEDx organization), so the rehearsal process could receive the attention it deserves and a successful talk would be an expected outcome instead of a long shot. Sometimes it's not so easy to see beyond the ego. But it's the key to making the right call.

It would have helped the speakers who haven't performed their best, if a curator would have said something like "Look, I completely believe in your idea worth spreading. And I believe in your ability to perform. It's just that there's not enough time left, and I don't want to put either of us through an overly stressed process. Let's put you on the list for our next event, so you can build the performance you truly want to give, and let you share the idea you want to share more than anything. And we'll be thrilled to see that. We grant you that time, please do the same for yourself."

Do not take any chances when it comes to copyright. Respect every artist's copyright policy.

Use an image that conveys your message, and make sure you have a right to use the artwork.
If you don't have that right,
don't use the image.

♥

MULTIMEDIA SHOCK THERAPY

Slides Stress

A tight rope. This had to be the metaphor to decribe the feeling I wanted to communicate in the first few minuteds of my talk. My sister and I had felt as is we were walking a tight rope since the moment we lost our parents and we became orphans. We felt as if we were walking at this incredible height, alone and without support. I wanted the best possible photograph to convey that emotion.

The hunt for the perfect picture representing this emotion was not easy. After some time, I found an amazing photo taken by Loomis Dean in 1952, of a Florida State University girl walking a tight rope. It was the absolute perfect picture for my presentation. It had the emotions of fear and admiration in it, and the perspective of a bystander. But the picture was published by LIFE magazine, which made it close to impossible to get permission to use it for my TEDx talk. And even if we would have received permission, the TEDx YouTube team wouldn't have published my talk on their global channel because of it. Using the amazing photograph would have definitely bitten me in the tail.

I can tell you that losing the opportunity to use this powerful photograph was a setback for me personally. Not only did I love the photograph, but it also completely illustrated the emotion that I was trying to bring across in the first few minutes of my talk. Copyright issues made using the picture impossible, the TEDx organization confirmed, not in this short time frame and with the available budget, anyway. I killed my visual darling and continued my hunt.

I stumbled upon the powerful image of Philippe Petit walking on a tight rope between the Twin Towers in New York

City in 1974. I had heard of this nerve-racking stunt before. The picture was fierce. There was no doubt in anyone's mind that Mr. Petit's amazing endeavour in New York City would paint the picture of the emotional challenge I was facing as a teenage orphan. But the same problem occurred: copyright. Then I knew that the only solution was to paint the picture verbally, carefully and deliberately. I decided to take on that challenge. This was the safest route. And I didn't want to use paid stock photography.

Frankly, I didn't want to use any visuals at all. Right then and there I realized: who needs slides anyway? I didn't. Well, not for this talk, anyway.

My speaker coaches confirmed my choice: no slides would be necessary for my talk. I was so relieved! However, after the next team meeting, this relief vanished into oblivion. The stage manager had stated that everyone should use slides, 'for visual impact and dramatic expression'. I disagreed, but after a short discussion I decided to put together a simple set of slides of keywords only. I also handed in some of my own art work, so that the stage management team could use those images as illustration material on the triangular screens in the auditorium. My only comment on this was: "As long as I don't have to hold the laser pointer. Follow my lead and flick through the slides as directed in the script." I decided not to give it any more thought. This felt right.

If I were to do it again, I probably wouldn't use slides at all, in order to focus on my own performance even more. But it worked out fine.

KEY TAKEAWAYS

Nothing more, nothing less

For TEDx Talks, you shouldn't need slides. Your story should be powerful enough to give the audience your message. For some topics, for instance large chunks of data with statistics, you might need slides. But by all means, keep them as simple as possible. No logos, no unnecessary visual clutter.

Use one slide per key word or idea. You'll want to avoid having your audience staring at your insanely wonderful graphics instead of listening to you making your point. Even worse: you're telling your story while peeking at your slides. If you do this, you distract your audience from your message. So don't do this.

Visual media can make or break you, and the basic design principle 'less is more' certainly is applicable for creating slides for a TEDx performance.

During the final rehearsals in the day(s) before the event, your stage management tests lighting, audio and visual aids, your head set, the battery for laser pointers (really) and correct plugging of power sockets and other technical gear, so you won't be unpleasantly surprised. You may be rolling your eyes while reading this ("Are you kidding me? Are you really advising me to not forget the power cable?"), but trust me: many presentations go haywire because of silly things like these. If your team doesn't talk about this when you think this should be discussed, bring it up yourself.

Always do a complete walk-through of your talk on the day before the event, including tech, audio, video, gear and everything. Present the whole thing.

In the years since my college graduation, I have written and designed thousands of presentation slides. Most of them were for presentations about social media and online communication, and also about my first book. Having a graphic insight and experience in chopping up large amounts of information into crunchy chunks, this all seemed very doable to me. And it was.

However, it proved to be a different game than the usual slide deck schtick.

I started with checking the slide decks of other TEDx and TED speakers. What were they sharing and how did they present facts and metaphors in their visual communication? Soon, the TEDx organization gave me tips (https://www.ted.com/participate/organize-a-local-tedx-event/tedx-organizer-guide/speakers-program/prepare-your-speaker/create-prepare-slides) for preparing my slide deck. I'll mention some of the tips provided by the TEDx organization.

For starters: only use slides that handle one specific point in your talk. Don't place too much information on one slide. Use high resolution visuals to avoid pixelated, messy slideshows. Use a simple background. Use a clear and straightforward font, such as Helvetica, Gill Sans or a variation.

Use the right dimensions for your slides (9:16 or 3:4) so there won't be any material falling off the screen. Skip unnecessary slides, because less is more.

Make sure you own the rights to of the images you use in your presentation (TED and TEDx will not publish any talk on YouTube that violates the rights of anyone who created artwork of any kind), or create your own art work.

From these tips, the last one appeared to be the most challenging. Since I planned to use some powerful metaphors, I knew I would probably bump into some copyright issues, because most metaphors are already widely interpreted visually by many people. So I realized that it would take more creativity. Fortunately, I have lots of that. I had to skip all the fluff and go back to basics. This lead to the following outcome: I verbally, not visually, loaded the metaphor I chose (walking on a tight rope).

The visuals I used in the stage design were details of m own art work from my journal. The stage manager chose details from those visuals, and my slide deck was as basic as could be: flat backgrounds, few words in capitals, some symbols. Nothing more. What I already knew did blossom in the end: I could carry the story all by myself. If the slides hadn't worked, that would have been fine, too. The other tips, I already knew, having studied graphic design and having crafted many slide decks. So my quest for the ultimate visual aid didn't end there. I discovered a very well crafted book written by Nancy Duarte, 'Slide:ology'. Nancy is also the author of 'Resonate' and 'The HBR Guide To Persuasive Presentations'. 'Slide:ology' is a very useful book for anyone who wants to create more captivating visual aids for presentations. She emphasizes the importance of communication and inspiration. Following Duarte's advice will help anyone improve their visual communication skills in order to present valuable stories. Why did I take Duarte's advice? For starters, she has a proven track record. She designed Al Gore's presentation slides for his Oscar-winning An Inconvenient Truth documentary.

In her book 'Resonate', Duarte teaches her readers the importance of focusing on content development methodologies that will move people to action. She also introduces the concept of storytelling persona techniques which make the audience the hero and the presenter the mentor. She does that by showing how to use story techniques of conflict and resolution in presentations. The result: engaging, captivating stories that you do not want to miss one word of.

The best stories created this way not only make the audience the hero, but they entice the audience to take action. Action heroes change the rules, move mountains and decide what comes next. Duarte teaches you to be the mentor, and to make each and every person in your audience feel like an action hero.

You can benefit from this knowledge. You could astart with checking your last presentation slide deck. Do your slides cover one information point per slide? Do your slides support your talk (that's what you'll want) or do they lead you through the talk (my advice: do not become the slave of any visual instrument)? Have you used a clear font like Helvetica or are you just too fond of Comic Sans? If you don't use proper typography, the TEDx organization will alter your slides anyway. As they should. Nobody wants a TEDx event with ugly typesetting. It would make you and your talk less credible. Bad design would reflect on the powerful TEDx brand. If you have any doubts about skipping Comic Sans for your presentation, please visit www.comicsanscriminal.com.

Customization commodity

Canva.com is an amazing online platform where you can create all kinds of visual materials, such as business cards, flyers, documents, posters, social media graphics, print materials and presentation slides. Canva is dear to me and I use it for many communication materials, including my presentations.

One of Canva's wonderful features is providing design templates that you can use and alter as you wish. This works very well for me, and it is a big time-saver for my business, as it is for many people. I have integrated my own corporate identity into my Canva templates, so that all my communication is recognizable as mine and/or my company's. I have a degree in Graphic & Interactive Design, so for me it's not too difficult to develop a visual identity and translate it to different kinds of communication materials, in sync with their purpose.

However, I have seen dreadful examples of standardized presentation slides gone wrong. Many people use Canva templates in a not-so-creative fashion. They either use the template and don't alter it in a way that helps their communication stand out from other people's creations. If many people use the same template, you instantly recognize their materials as being standardized Canva solutions. Don't get me wrong, I love Canva and its templates. But customizing a template is as logical and necessary as having your own clothing style that suits you and your features best. Or creating your own unique atmosphere in your home.

Perhaps you wear an I Love NY t-shirt, combined with your own unique blazer or hand made skirt. Perhaps you bought your couch at IKEA, but placed hand made pillows on it. You use recognizable images and then make them your own by adding something unique to YOU.

Creating visual identity is about finding out who you really are and what you want to associate yourself with. It's showing what you feel comfortable with and is an extension of your unique personality. Usually, that means combining your unique taste and a standardized commodity. The same goes for creating slide decks on Canva. Go with a template, but customize it so your audience or clients can recognize what you wish to communicate in a way it suits you and your message. This also helps funnel the right people you want to communicate with and sifts out people with whom your message doesn't resonate very well.

It's natural selection at the gate. Be mindful of your visual choices for your presentation slide deck, for it may attract or repel people.

After you have decided what your message is and how you want to bring it across, you can go on to making the presentation you'll want to use at Your Talk. The next step is crafting a slide for every one of your Walking The Talk cards (the cards you used to craft your talk and that you had to reduce to about ten pieces).

This means that you'll have about ten slides for your entire presentation. This should be more than enough. You may want to add one or two slides, if the message or image on them adds to the power of the intended effect on your audience.

Slides And Timing
One of the TED talks I found entertaining and illustrative of the power of slides and timing was 'The Worst-Designed Thing You've Never Noticed', performed by Roman Mars. He shaped his performance into a radio-like show, sitting behind a desk with a desk top microphone, a sound deck and an iPad with pre-recorded voices that he cued when necessary.

His topic was about flag design, and what could possibly go wrong in designing a flag. Roman showed his slides at exactly the right moments to trigger laughter in the audience. Roman Mars integrated his sense of humor, his expertise and the power of timing in his talk.

"Always make sure
the direction of your picture
is towards your text, not away.
Otherwise it looks you don't really
believe what you are saying.

An image can confirm or deny
your message.
Make sure it's the former,
not the latter."

—Else Kramer

INTERVIEW

Else Kramer:

"Visuals are essential in engaging your audience but make sure they aligh with your core message and brand identity."

Else Kramer is a Visual Revolutionary. She helps business leverage the power of visual marketing through speaking, in-company training, campaigns and consulting. www.visualrevolutionaries.com

Else, the importance of visuals in presentations is evident. Or are there speaking scenarios in which visuals are unnecessary?
I believe that there are some outstanding speakers that can manage without visual aids. But I also know that a percentage of the audience will be visual learners. Why not help them along? In addition to increasing retention in your audience, you can create more layers of meaning by using visuals, and you can evoke more emotion.

When crafting a presentation, what is the best way to choose a visual theme?
This depends on two things. The first thing you have to ask yourself is: what do you want to achieve, what do you want your audience to experience and learn? The second thing is your brand identity. You can't skip either. Ideally, you'll find the perfect way to blend them.

Start with your core message—the main point you want to make. Think about what kind of picture you want to evoke with your keynote. Is it bright? Cheerful? Black and white? Is it highly stylised or more organic? Use this 'vision' as a starting point when you select or create your visuals.

Do you have a set template for your presentations?
Yes, I do. I always have consistency and alignment with my brand identity. And though I love to use Lego to illustrate my point I don't always use it, this depends both on topic and on audience.

You're quite well-known for using Lego in your visuals - how did that start?
Well, I was looking for a specific style and models to illustrate a course I was teaching. But it was very hard to find a timeless, classic style. I already loved Lego, so I decided to work with that and use Lego minifigures as my models. This turned out to be an incredibly popular choice. People love it. Lego is designed so well—it gives everyone a kind of canvas on which to project their own stories.

What do you prefer in a keynote: variation or consistency in visuals?
It totally depends. I'm pretty lenient: I think you should use whatever is most effective in getting your message across, in connecting with your audience. With that said: I'm also a sucker for consistency. The best keynotes combine very effective visuals with great style and consistency.

If you were to present or speak about visual marketing, without the possibility of using visuals, how would you do this?
If I had to speak about visual marketing without visuals, I'd feel severely handicapped. I would dance, probably! I'd do anything that's visually triggering. Draw in the air, paint with a laser presenter. And of course I'd use very vivid, evocative language. Which by the way is always a good idea—whether you use visuals or not.

What kind of presentations do you give the most? Instructions, workshops, vision, trends, or something else?
I give interactive keynotes, trend talks, inspirational sessions, trainings—to groups ranging from 10 to over a 1,000 people. Whatever the format or size of the audience it's all about engaging

and connecting. Your audience gives you something incredibly precious: their time. It's your job as a speaker to leave them feeling enriched afterwards.

Else, you have presented in the Netherlands, in Spain, in Poland and you have undoubtedly more ambitions for speaking abroad. Do you feel there is a difference in the way people from various cultures respond to your visuals?
Not so much in terms of visuals, but the level and amount of interactions will absolutely vary in different countries. I'm not too worried about using Lego in international presentations, because it's neutral and pretty inoffensive. But I can imagine visuals going wrong in different cultures. Just think about the symbolic meaning of white in China: it means death. And you don't want to have people drinking on pictures in Saudi Arabia. So you always have to craft your keynote with your audience in mind.

Is there anything else you'd like to share on visual communication and marketing for speakers?
Use more images. And look for a fit with your brand. Microsoft uses polished images that are consistent with their brand. But if you're an entrepreneur or a solopreneur, please feel free to have a personal touch, and use images you used yourself. It will move people more than stock photography could ever do.

Who inspires you?
Andy Puddicombe, the founder of Headspace, the meditation app. I love the way they use animations and visuals in their app to make meditation more accessible. And I love that Andy and his team are getting hundreds of thousands of people around the world to meditate and have better lives!

And I also admire Scott Belsky, the founder of Behance, he is a great driver and enabler of creativity, and helps creatives to go beyond the idea level, and realise their vision.

What is your biggest pet peeve in visual presentation materials?
Uninspiring stock photography and bullet points.

Releasing your script at the right moment can be liberating.

FEEDBACK

Let Go Of What You're Afraid To Lose

Three weeks before the TEDx conference, the TEDx committee advised me to stop rehearsing for fourteen days. "You are over trained. You know everything already, but you seem stressed out and forced, which blurs your message. Stop rehearsing and start doing other fun things." While intrinsically screaming 'Are You Out Of Your Mind!?', I accepted their advice. As much as I didn't want to leave things be, somewhere deep inside, I knew they were right. I then managed to leave the script for ten days. Being an insufferable control freak, this was challenging.

So I went on trips, bought a dress to wear on stage, went to the zoo, petted my cat, visited friends and watched all Star Wars movies. Twice. Of course, I grinned when I heard the character of Master Yoda say: "Train Yourself To Let Go Of Everything You Fear To Lose".

It was a good call that I took my coaches' wise advice. Two weeks later, I rehearsed one more time in front of the committee. The whole thing came naturally. I was ready.

The ego appeases your mind, thinking you are the smartest one in the room.
Perhaps you are.
But you might discover new insights. You'll indeed be the smartest in the room if you give yourself the chance to internalize those fresh insights as fast as you can.

KEY TAKEAWAYS

Trust The Process

One of the most difficult things for many people to learn, is to deal with feedback gracefully. That's understandable. It's easier to hear that we're doing a good job than getting remarks about our performance. But if you want to up your game, you'll have to make it easy for other people to share their feedback with you. Stay open to the idea that other people might know more about something than you do and try not to judge the feedback. Take the advice into consideration and trust that they have your best interest at heart. Play with their suggestions during rehearsals, live with them for a while. Give yourself the opportunity to enhance your performance.

To stay open to feedback and to learn in a practical way, you might have to battle some intrinsic demons. Insecurities, perhaps. Or the contrary, convictions you're already mastering all of this. The ego often thinks you're the smartest in the room. Perhaps you are. But you might discover new insights. You will be the smartest in the room if you give yourself the chance to internalize those insights as fast as you can. Letting your ego lead the way in your presentation equals shooting yourself in the foot. When was the last time you were inspired by a speaker who was self-absorbed and who made you feel less-than? Don't be that person. Stay open to feedback. And turn Your Weaknesses Into Strengths.

Stuttering
Did you know many public speakers have had (or still have) a stutter? Sounds strange, right? Would you believe me if I told you that Marilyn Monroe had a stutter from time to time? It was trauma induced. I wrote about it in the chapter 'V-v-verbal exp-p-pression' in my first book 'So, You're An Orphan Now'. On YouTube (search 'Marilyn Monroe stutter'), you can find Marilyn's quote about her stuttering.

Dealing with the appearance of your fear doesn't make it go away. Dealing with the underlying issue does. Approach your issue with curiosity. It may be a blessing in disguise.

'The first time was at the orphanage, and then later, in my teens I stuttered. And then I was...ehm...they elected me secretary of the English class, and ehm, then I had to say "minute of the last meeting", but I went "mmmhh-mmmhh-mmmhh." (laughs) Oh, it's terrible. When? After the orphanage, when I was thirteen, I took it up again. I don't know how it happened, I just stuttered. Sometimes, when I'm very nervous or excited or something, I stutter. And in fact one time, I had a small part in a movie and ehm, ehm, the director came to me and yelled at me. Oh, he talked awful. And he "vrrrRRHrrwwwhh-hOOOH"-ed at me. And when I got into the scene, instead of my lines, I "woo-woo-woo"-ed, and the director came at me. He was furious and said: "YOU don't stutter!" I said: "That's what YOU think!" (laughs) "Oh, it's painful, oh God!"
- Marilyn Monroe

I've had a stutter since I was about eleven years old. It was also trauma induced. The last years of my parents' lives weren't peaceful, and the shock of losing them when they died, left me slightly verbally impaired. Literally. I did not get half a sentence out of my mouth without a staccato cannonade of stuttering. At moments of frustration, even curse words came out one letter at a time. This felt as if the letters shot back at me. Looking back, it was a striking metaphor for my emotions. Overwhelmed, and I didn't have words to express myself. I was silenced by grief.

    Years later, at the art academy, I re-learned to express myself adequately. By making designs, but more importantly, during the mandatory presentations to explain design concepts. It often seemed like 'defending oneself', and that's what it often came down to. They set high standards at the academy. It was quite demanding. The more reviews and presentations I endured, the easier it became for me. I gritted it out and became a better presenter. Also singing lessons helped me breathe intentionally and to become a bit more relaxed.

    One of the key elements that helped me overcome most of my stuttering, was realising that stuttering wasn't necessary anymore. Nobody was silencing me, least of all me. I had earned my place in life and career. I could release myself of the discomfort.

Today, speaking is the core of my work. I share knowledge and experience about topics such as online communication strategy, social media, e-learning, video conferences and livestreaming. I have made hundreds of video instructions, podcasts, online video interviews and screencasts for my students and clients. And whenever I do, whether it's one-on-one, online or in a room with hundreds of people, I am part of them, and they are part of me. That relationship is a close one.

Sometimes, I still stutter. It rarely happens on stage. But when I feel a stutter coming up, I take a breath (as everybody does), find a synonym and continue where I left of. Pausing for just a second reels the audience in. They listen with even more attention. In that aspect, it actually is a blessing in disguise. When I stutter in informal settings or when I'm with friends, one of my dearest friends always says: "Oh girl. That's just one of your charms."

"Tha-tha-thanks man."

Accents

If you have an accent, then accept that you're different from the rest. And trust that they will still want to hear your valuable message. A tip though: try to keep up your fluency in language. Adjust your pronunciation to the public you're speaking with. For instance: I am from the Netherlands, and Dutch is my native language. I do have a slight accent when I speak English. I don't mind having an accent, but I do try to adjust my pronunciation. I want to feel as comfortable as possible in conversations. My accent still shines through. I don't mind.

Language is a living thing, and you can express yourself in many ways. In my TEDx talk, my pronunciation sometimes sounds a bit British, sometimes a bit American. And I even used an Irish expression. Perhaps I could've worked on that a bit more. I guess you speak what influences you. I haven't heard anybody complain about not being able to understand what I was saying.

Practicing is important to me. I get myself in the speaking arena with people in the UK, US and Ireland almost on a daily basis. I want to be able to express myself freely. And I often ask the people I'm in a conversation with, how they experience my English.

I recently was in a the featured Blabnation show with Jonathan Tripp, on Blab.im. Jonathan lives in the US, and he answered my question: "It isn't distracting." That's enough to be able to speak abroad with confidence. Not training to improve my speaking every day would rob me of opportunities to engage with other experts all over the world. Just the thought that I'd only be able to speak in my own country in my own language throughout my career…it just doesn't feel right. I love my country and my language. It's colourful. It feels like home. But the world is bigger than your own country. Stretch your words, stretch your world. In the world of TEDx, most people have an accent, because it's so international. To me, its part of the charm and the feeling of being connected.

Insecurity about your looks
If you feel insecure about your appearance, then you might hire a stylist, to choose clothing, make-up and a hairdo that emphasize your good features. Just remember that confidence comes from within. But you can give it a nudge.

Crowds
If you get intimidated by large crowds, then rehearse speaking in informal settings. Choose bigger crowds of people every time. Level up and stretch your boundaries and comfort zone. Start working with a performance coach to get you more comfortable.

Curiosity Is Key
The key in flipping your alleged weaknesses into strenghts, is to stay open to those fears, without letting them paralyze you. Get to know your fears as if they were your friends. Don't avoid them. Instead, give them a place in your world and live with them.

Reduce your fears to human proportions. Dive into what these fears stand for. Usually, fear of someone or something boils back to an underlying fear or insecurity, that's causing unwelcome symptoms. Dealing with the appearance of your fear doesn't make it go away. Dealing with the underlying issue does. Approach your issue with curiosity. It may be a blessing in disguise.

"Life is short.
Make it deep."

—Buffi Duberman

INTERVIEW

Buffi Duberman:

"Rock Your English!"

Buffi Duberman is a native New Yorker who has spent more than half her life coaching non-native English speakers in the use of their English. She has been living in the Netherlands for over twenty-five years. Over the last 15 years, she has become a household name as the Personal English Coach (a business that she created) to the hottest artists, CEO's and entrepreneurs. Her book 'Rock Your English!' is available in the Netherlands, Norway and Belgium.

This book was followed by her two online courses 'Rock Your English @ Home!' and www.businessenglishcommunication.com. Her new book '100 Ways To Save Your Ass In English' is about how to improve your English in a fresh and funky way for all kinds of professional situations. Buffi has also been an official TEDxAmsterdam speaker coach for years. She coaches performers for television shows such as The Voice Of Holland and So You Wanna Be A Popstar.

She helps artists write better lyrics. Buffi also coaches actors, CEO's and politicians in media training and presentation skills. National newspaper Volkskrant wrote in an interview that artists call her 'Buffi The Accent Slayer'. The NRC called her personality "disruptively compassionate".

Buffi, you are a specialist in teaching non-native English speaking people how to improve their English. How do you start the coaching process for TEDx speakers?
I start by asking them what their message is—what does their heart want to say to the hearts of the audience? And what are they afraid of when it comes to this particular presentation? Once we identify their story, and identify and tackle their fears, then we can start shaping and sharing their story with the world!

What are the first things you notice in their use of the English language that have to be tackled as soon as possible?
Usually it's pronunciation. Once the message is clear, then we talk about how to deliver it - and pronunciation is not just the sounds that come out of your mouth - it's also about delivery, timing, flow, emphasis, etc. And then body language kicks in!

How do you feel about hearing a Dutch accent in a TEDx talk? Is it horrible, or isn't it as bad as we tend to think?
People are often unaware of a few things - the two different kinds of TH (how this letter combination sounds), the difference between US and UK English (which usually gets mixed up throughout the talk), and the connection between words. I coach the speakers to speak with ease and confidence. If they slip up on their pronunciation from time to time, that's ok as they will still be connected to their audience if they speak from the heart and stay true to themselves and their story.

Do you help TEDx speakers enrich their vocabulary to make their talk resonate more with the audience?
Yes, absolutely! You need to have all the colours of the world at your disposal when you are painting a picture. The same goes for your words. I work hard to make sure the words they choose really reflect what they mean. Sometimes the first choice is not the best choice...or the easiest one!

Every language has its own colourful, metaphoric expressions. Sometimes, non-native English speakers translate these expressions to English, without checking to see if there is an expression in English for the same phenomenon. We have seen this for instance with Dutch politicians who are pleading their case abroad. This often leads to raised eyebrows at the receiving end.

How do you deal with mistakes like these with your students?
First I laugh (as I did when someone called me 'an excellent cock' after I made him dinner), then I give them my business card. (laughs) It all depends on the context. Louis van Gaal gets away with murder due to his lack of good English; he uses that to his

full advantage, and it really works for him! In many European countries, English has found its way into people's lives through television, the Internet and via other sources. Also many high schools provide dual language education.

Is this helpful in raising the quality of English language in European countries with other primary languages? Or does this depend on the level of expertise of the teachers in those schools?
I think a lot of this has to do with the teacher. So many teachers have been teaching the same old story for far too long and have lost their connection with their students and youth culture. That's why I use music in my lessons—to keep it fresh and fun(ky). It works! And many people have a false idea about their English due to being exposed to so much English around them. Just because they understand it, does not mean that they can use it naturally and spontaneously. The ears usually know more than the mouth.

What do you never wish to hear again, in terms of non-native people speaking English?
Someone speaking from fear and trying 'just to get it over with' - we feel that right away and it's such a shame as it can be corrected with coaching. So many people feel that they have no stories to tell because they don't value themselves. We need to realise how awesome we all are and that everyone has a story to share with the world. Sometimes you have to dig deep to hit gold, but it's there.

Could you recommend a language exercise that would help most non-native English speakers and give them a head start?
Talk as much as you can, get feedback, and apply that feedback. And buy my books and my online course if you want to have fun learning!

Is there anything you'd like to add?
Life is short. Make it deep.

Public Speaking Shouldn't Be A Cathartic Exercise.

Period.

EMOTIONS IN YOURSELF AND IN YOUR TALK

Think Silently For Yourself

After I had decided how to connect and interact with the audience in the TEDx format—where there isn't room to have a conversation with one or two people in the audience—the construction of my talk became clear. But I was still searching for a way to let people have some space with their own emotions about the facts that I was going to share with them. I came up with this:

"I'm not going for transference. I don't want them to feel my emotions. I want them to feel their own emotions."

Unraveling my own mixed emotions about my personal history on one hand, and losing my foster dad on the other hand, was something I knew I didn't want to burden my audience with. So I came up with a way for people to deal with their own thoughts while, at the same time, urging them to project my story onto their own lives.

The solution was to create a sacred moment of silence during my talk. A moment that would provide people in the audience some space to think of what they would wish for their own children.

A fragment of my talk zooms in on the hypothetical scenario of a person sitting in the audience having been in a car accident. "You have had some bad luck, you were in a car accident. And you're gone. The person who is sitting next to you, right here in this room, is still alive. And you get one last chance to pass on a message to your child, through that person sitting next to you. Now, please look at one another, and think silently to yourself: what would your message for your child be?"

I haven't counted exactly how long the silence lasted.

I think it's about eight or nine seconds at least. A bit longer than most people might consider comfortable. But I felt it was necessary, since I didn't want to rush people.

Then I said: "I'd like to believe that what you are thinking right now is inspiration for living."

The silence gave the audience the opportunity to integrate the situation and to connect this with their feelings for their own children. It was functional. And if I had it to do over again today, I would.

After this interactive intermezzo, I went back to sharing what had happened to me after my parents had died, and how I met my future foster parents. I felt it was of vital importance to guide the audience through the emotions and then take them back to the safety of my story, instead of leaving them in their own emotions for their children. A speaker who shares a story that may trigger emotions should carry the responsibility to bring the audience full circle. Back where they were, in the same safety zone as they were in when you first started speaking. I took that responsibility very seriously. Because it's the right thing to do, but also because I wanted people to act proactively, in a positive way, when they encountered a bereaved child at some point in their lives. It was a very intensely positive mission. And it still is.

KEY TAKEWAYS

Lead The Way

Sharing a personal story about, for instance, overcoming adversity, means you are letting people into your world, your personal space. You have to be a good host and your guests should behave accordingly. Being a good host in the world of your story means that you guide people through emotions and don't leave them hanging. Leaving people in a dark or vulnerable place when you're wrapping up your talk is cruel. And it is counterproductive. You can't leave your audience in a dark place and then expect them to take your message and do something with it in their lives.

Being a good story host means that you take your guests along through emotions and experiences, being graceful enough to end the story cycle so that they feel well-treated, complete and positive. This does not mean you can't share confrontational facts, vivid words, or a dark sense of humor. Being colourful in your story helps people paint the picture of your story in their minds. But finishing positively (or constructively) helps them integrate your message.

Being a good host to people with your emotions
During the writing process for my TEDx talk, I not only realized that I had to translate my own emotions into words that would resonate, but I also knew that I had to guide my audience through some emotions as well. This was my responsiblity as a speaker.

Fortunately, I had worked through my personal emotions that lead to me speaking at TEDx years beforehand. If I hadn't worked through them, I wouldn't have been able to share freely on stage. I strongly believe that public speaking and sharing personal experiences should never, ever be a cathartic exercise for the speaker. But it might be a cathartic experience for the audience.

You may share confrontational facts, vivid words, or a dark sense of humor.
Being colourful in your story helps people paint the picture of your story in their minds. But make sure you finish positively and constructively. This helps your audience integrating your message.

Getting Personal For Educational Purposes
Since I have been through growing up without my parents from the age of fourteen, I have encountered just about every kind of human reaction to this fact. And I feel that it's my moral responsibility to provide today's children with a tool to teach people how they would want to be treated, and to provide the people around them with ways connect with bereaved children. I discovered that sharing my own personal, true story was the right way to go about it. So sharing my story was a cerebral choice, from a purely educational motive.

Just before and during the first two years after the book was published, I had spoken a lot about the topic, in order to raise awareness about orphaned children in Western society. I felt comfortable talking about this and I felt comfortable about my own experiences. I felt at ease, because my motives were crystal clear.

Sometimes I see people speak of their personal experiences and intense topics. Often, I get the impression that the moment that they had decided to share their story could have been chosen more wisely. Not that the topic should remain a taboo - far from it. But if the person sharing the story hasn't worked through his or her own complex emotions about this, the speaker could unintentionally hijack the audience to a space they don't really want to be in.

Public Speaking Shouldn't Be A Cathartic Exercise. Period.
I believe it's ethically irresponsible and unwise to let other people be part of your personal psychological process. This is an environment that you are responsible for. You have to work through your own emotions and experiences. You can't burden other people with this. They would probably feel that you are over-sharing and making them witnesses to your personal saga. The stage is never, ever a therapeutic session. Never.

When I turned twenty-eight, I struggled with burnout that lasted five months, burn-out due to unprocessed grief about that huge loss in my childhood. I decided to work with a personal coach to integrate the feelings of loss and to find new energy and inspiration to build the rest of my life. This was a wise decision, because working through these emotions has brought me a lot.

Almost ten years after that, I decided to share my story in a book. I wasn't planning on sharing my personal story publicly at all, but I realized that if I wanted things to change for today's bereaved children in the Western world, I had to open up and share my own, true story. I knew that sharing a fictional story wouldn't be as powerful. And I didn't feel that I had anything to hide. I didn't have any reason to feel shame about my past. It was a part of who I was, and I was cool with that. Understanding what a child is going through after his or her parents pass away at an early age is quite difficult. It's even more challenging to think of what to say to a bereaved child. I wanted to provide a solution.

When It's Out There
The publication of my book lead to many interviews in newspapers, women's magazines, national news networks, radio shows and more. I couldn't have done this in a professional way if I hadn't sorted through my emotions and if I didn't know my purpose for sharing the story, which was to change things for today's orphaned children. And it started to work, because many people have responded to the story by changing something for children in their environment. This is an ongoing issue, because there will always be children who are struggling with the loss and grief of losing loved ones.

There are two sides to the issue of sharing a personal story publicly. Both are equally important, in my opinion. There is the perspective of you protecting yourself and your story from people who do not have the right to be part of it. Shame researcher Brené Brown wrote in her book 'The Gifts of Imperfection': "Our stories are not meant for everyone. Hearing them is a privilege, and we should always ask ourselves this before we share: "Who has earned the right to hear my story?" I completely agree with this. You should be cautious with sharing, expecially if it is a vulnerable story.

Do Not Overshare

Then there's the perspective of finding the balance between being vulnerable in a powerful way and the trap of oversharing. Brené Brown writes in her book Daring Greatly: "Oversharing is not vulnerability. In fact, it often results in disconnection, distrust and disengagement." Again, I completely agree. There is a piercing difference between sharing in a vulnerable way in order to achieve a certain purpose, and over-sharing and making other people feel uncomfortable, leaving them uncertain what to do with the information and emotion waterfall you have dumped on them.

I believe that for some public speakers, it might have been better if they had waited to share their story, and instead first sorted out their emotions and story purpose. This shows more respect for yourself and for your audience. Aim for that.

Professional stories with a personal touch

For other, less personal stories that you want to resonate with your audience's hearts and minds, it's wise to add a personal touch. A wonderful and excellent example of a professional TEDx talk about a certain medical procedure is Edward Valstar's talk. His talk, 'Joined At The Hip', was about an innovative procedure for treating osteoarthritis. Edward stated in his talk: "Every year, one and a half million people in the world are treated for osteoarthritis with hip prosthesis. Our aim is to make these hip replacements last for a lifetime." He illustrated the importance of this innovation by mentioning that his grandmother had suffered from the same condition, and how enormous the positive impact of such a treatment would be on her life. Edward's choice to mention his grandmother was wise, because most people know about the discomforts elderly people have.

Everybody has a grandmother (whether or not they're alive). You can relate to the story, and therefore are more willing to listen to the novelties about this hip procedure.

In case of a professional talk like Edward's, a personal anchor point (his grandmother) often is enough. The trap of over-sharing personal infomation is less probable in this setting.

"It's an amazing gift
to yourself if you grant
yourself the experience
of failing miserably
in a safe environment
and to receive
quality feedback."

—Amy van Son

INTERVIEW

Amy van Son:

"Standing on that red dot was a life-changing moment"

Amy van Son is Licensee TEDxArnhem, online communication strategist, social careercoach and founder of the Your Song project.

Amy, how did you experience sharing your story at the TEDxGroningen conference?
I had shared my story before, on another occasion. But sharing it on a TEDx stage was shorter and much more intense. I also chose another way to tell the story. It wasn't as much about me, as it was about the underlying issue, illustrated by other people's experiences. And I didn't avoid my own story either. This was also a big thing for me, because I had kept my personal story inside until I was forty years old.

It was not until I started studying at the University of Humanistic Studies, that I had fully explored all aspects of my story and what this could mean for other people, for instance, for soldiers. I have a professional history in the Dutch army, and I grew up with it. Many soldiers are used to keeping their story inside, no matter how intense and sometimes horrible these stories can be. With all possible consequences. I wanted to make a difference for them, and in a way, also for me.

It has been an intense experience. Because you can ponder on which exact words to include in your story, but there's always the moment that your audience will interpret them. And a TEDx audience is big. And your talk will be available online forever. You can only hope that it works out the way you intended.

TEDxGroningen organiser Melissa Oudshoorn-Fuller had contacted me. She had heard about my project 'Your Song'. She challenged me to put the story on paper, in order to perform at their next conference. The only complication was that it was only six week before the event. That made preparing for the event stressful. If I could do it again, I would have taken more time to rehearse, perhaps even requesting a stage moment at a next conference, instead of stretching myself to almost unattainable goals.

What was the moment you were worried about most?
There were three things troubling me. I was performing with a pianist and a singer. I chose to do this, because I felt this combination would add to the experience for the audience, in order to fully grasp the essence of my idea worth spreading. Before the event, I was worried about the pianist. It was of vital importance that he'd started playing at the right moment. He started a few seconds later. And also Maame, my singer, entered the stage a tad too late. But in the end, that wasn't necessarily a bad thing. I shouldn't have worried about that, but I understand why I did.

The second thing that was troubling me happened right at the beginning of the performance. I looked at the clock, seconds ticking away. Four, five, six, seven... I had to perform, and for some unclear reason, I couldn't get into the flow of the story. I felt like a bunny on the highway. There I was, I had to do something, but I froze. It was a scary moment. Once I got into the story, things went better.

The third issue was that a bit further along during my talk, I heard myself saying things I had planned to while crafting the talk. I elaborated on what it's like to leave your home for six months to go on a military mission. At one point, I say: " Can you imagine embarking on a ship, going on a mission for six months, knowing you would finally be left alone." With these words, I felt the immense relief I had felt when I had experienced it myself, when I was much younger. I felt so relieved to be away from my own home back then, for it hadn't been a happy home. I also felt the sadness of the fact that leaving was the only way to find peace. I was just overwhelmed. That was when I lost the rhythm in speaking on stage. I felt alone with my story, while I was speaking to the audience. During rehearsals, I had thought: I'm such a part of this story, It'll work out fine. But this wasn't what happened at the moment supreme. I probably was also being too hard on myself. I expected myself to give a better performance, because I had spoken on stages so many times before. Along the way, I did return to the story. But it has been challenging. It wasn't all bad, though! And I'm glad I did it. Sharing the story gave me the opportunity to reshape my history, in order to live a fuller life. In a way, it has been cathartic. But I suppose the performance would have gone better if I had had more time to rehearse. The key: practice, practice, practice. And taking the time to live through the whole palette of emotions, when you're still in the safe zone of rehearsals.

I would advise every TEDx organiser to work with excellent speaker coaches. Every aspiring TEDx speaker should work with a speaker coach. Especially seasoned speakers can be somewhat stubborn in terms of the practical way they're rehearsing their performance. When you're used to being on stage, it can be a big surprise—not in a good way—to discover that speaking at a TEDx conference is something entirely different than you have encountered before. Some professional speakers tend to underestimate this endeavour. They shouldn't.

It's an amazing gift to yourself if you grant yourself the experience of failing miserably in a safe environment and to receive quality feedback. Don't ever fall in the trap of believing you don't need feedback for your TEDx talk. Your talk and performance need to mature, also to release the story and to perform it in a natural way. And if you feel you don't have enough time or you could do a better job than you are: dare to cancel. This is also what I have internalized since I've become the organiser of TEDxArnhem. My own experience has helped me recognize the phases the speakers are in.

What was the most exceptional moment of that whole day?
There was this fantastic post on Facebook, written by a girl from

Ukraine. She grew up in the political turmoil in that area, and went to college in Groningen in the Netherlands. She had listened to my talk, and she replied: "This talk has changed my life." She was intrigued by the war, and by the comment she was getting while growing up: "War is not for girls." Up until she had heard my talk, she had dressed as a boy. And now she lives according to her belief: "War indeed is not for just any woman. War is for educated women." She learned to accept herself as a young woman who wanted to be a war reporter. I'm glad I could contribute to her mind shift.

What happened in the following months?
The moment you are on the red dot, you realize it's also a life changing moment. Right after the event, I thought: why doesn't my home town have a TEDx conference?" I wanted to bring this experience to my own community. The whole package. The value of the time slot that is attributed to you, in which you are challenged to share your story. Choosing your tone of voice, pondering on what to share, what not to share. All these things have consequences for the final result. Because you don't know how you've performed until you've left the stage. I wanted more people in my own community to experience this process while sharing ideas worth spreading.

The TEDx concept is the only concept that has proven to cross borders in niches, age and social status. In the Netherlands, for many years, there's been this movement called Loesje. They print quotes on posters and hang them all over the country. One of the quotes they published was: "The best password is 'hi!'." For me, the best password is 'TEDx'. It opens doors to many possibilities and it teaches you how to organize multidisciplinary. That's what I'm good at. In my project Your Song, I had built bridges between seemingly different worlds. Organizing TEDxArnhem was the next logical step for me.

Do you recognize your emotions in the preparation or stage performances of the TEDxArnhem speakers?
It wouldn't be fair to generalize their performances, as each is unique. But the connecting factor is that the wish and determination to perform the best you possibly can. In some cases, this results in perfectionism, which can be counterproductive. I also recognize the relief once a performance is completed. You're leaving the stage. You've done it. You have done something you hadn't done before.

What do you advise aspiring speakers in terms of dealing with being emotional overwhelmed?
Prepare the best way you possibly can. Breathe in, breathe out. And repeat. Be grounded. I have watched social psychologist Amy Cuddy's TED talk about body language. Amy shares very useful advice in her talk. For instance, that standing in a 'high-power' pose for as little as two minutes can stimulate higher levels of testosterone and lower levels of cortisol (also known as the stress hormone).

I always make sure to mention her talk to the speakers that are on the lineup for TEDxArnhem. Furthermore, I'd like to emphasize that your talk is about your idea and your audience. You are 'just' the messenger. And don't ever underestimate the intelligence of your audience.

Is there anything else you'd like to share?
Organizing a TEDx event stretches your comfort zone and it gives you many things. The actual production may be a matter of skills and drills, the technical facilities. But a TEDx event is different from other events because you are truly building a relationship with everyone involved. A small example that illustrates this feeling: speakers, production team members and sponsors are all invited to the speaker's dinner, the evening before the actual event. And the speakers also connect with the audience, after performing. It's just a strong connection and a very special occasion.

COURAGE AND STAGE FRIGHT

Now That I'm Here

You know that last moment before something great happens? Often, that moment is filled with utter panic.

"You're on in twenty minutes. Please go to the audio technicians to get you wired up with mic gear."
Oh no. What if I forget everything? There was something with a postcard. What was that thing that I had to do with a postcard? Oh yes. It's in my pocket. Opening of the talk. What was my first sentence again? Oh, right. But what if break down and cry? Or stutter? I can't let that happen. I really, really can't. Too much emotion would distract the audience from my idea worth spreading. "Please let the idea land the right way", I hear myself mumbling. The idea, that is part of myself, but that has a right to exist by itself as well. It is powerful.

In the eleven years I have been speaking professionally, I never had stage fright. Healthy jitters in the last minutes before a performance, yes. Of course. But fear? No. Small rooms, large rooms, I love them all dearly. But here I am. Trembling hands, shaking limbs. Just like some of the other speakers here at TEDxDelft. I leave the Green Room and I pace across the room, with chattering teeth. I gaze out the enormous window. It looks out on the ceme-tery where we buried Coen, just two months before this day. A trumpeter played The Last Post. Only fifty steps from the stage where I will give my TEDx talk about his good deeds in my life, he lies in his grave. So far away, so close.

"Fifteen minutes!"
I was just there this morning, at his grave. I burned a candle. Promised him once more that the world would hear how he and his wife helped me when I needed it most.

You can't imagine
just how excruciatingly
scary and wonderfully
thrilling that red dot
on the floor can be,
if you haven't walked
towards it in real life.

That anyone can help an orphan, and how exactly they can do so. Promised him once more that I wouldn't overreact, that I would just do it. When my first book was published, I almost choked up because Coen was there. It touched my heart seeing him there, because without him, the book wouldn't have been written. But now I choke up because Coen won't be here today. The last times with, become the first times without.

But my TEDx talk isn't about death. It is about life.

"Come on, you chicken. What are you lingering here for? Go on, do it!", I hear Coen say in my head. And he is right.

"Ten minutes!"
I dial Ric's number. My director and dear friend. "Help, I don't know what to do anymore!" "Jo, we're sitting here, all of us, ready for the livestream." "Yeah, but I'm stuck! I just don't know where to start anymore!" "Jo. Come on. You can totally do this. We have been practicing for months. Do you remember the ten steps in the story? The ten cards?" "Yeah." "You see. You will nail this. Go on. I'll hear you on the other side. I'm proud of you already. Good luck!" His words are soothing. They help me get my act together.

"Five minutes, backstage please!"
Someone wiggles a microphone deep down in my dress. I start visualizing my father on the left hand side of the audience in the packed auditorium. I give my mother her place in the centre, top row. Coen, my foster dad, has his place on the right hand side.
This room has twelve hundred seats, but twelve hundred and three people are present. My foster mom is here, alive and well. I'm so grateful she is here. My nerves shoot through my body like a pinball machine. But the room is my home, for my loved ones are here. I can feel it.

"Time. Go get 'em!"
I speak. Sixteen minutes and twenty-one seconds later, I know that it has been worth all the effort.

"Of course it's happening in your head, Harry, but why should that mean it's not real?"

—Albus Dumbledore, *Harry Potter and the Deathly Hallows*, J.K. Rowling

KEY TAKEAWAYS

Of Course It's Happening Inside Your Head

Glossophobia. That's the official word for stage fright. I have a hunch you couldn't care less what it's called when you're busy managing your brains' amygdala punk rock party while clenching your sweaty palms, trying to lower your heart rate and avoiding the urge to vomit in the nearest potted plant, just minutes before your stage manager calls you to the stage.

Maybe you're not thinking at all. Perhaps you're suffering from black-out, or you're too busy water-managing your outfit. Or you're just whispering a mantra about this whole gig being over as quickly as humanly possible.

Whether you're going to be on stage speaking about your latest brilliant ground-breaking invention or you're about to tell a personal story with the intention of sharing it with the whole world, chances are that you'd like to have your loved ones there with you. Your parents, spouse, children perhaps.

You want your audience to take your key message with them so they can change a little piece in their world for the better. Your loved ones are part of you and of the whole world. But having your loved ones near during your stage performance can be as soothing as it can be intensely stressful. They know you very well, on good days and on bad ones. You think they'll see right through you when you're out there. And yes, they probably will. But they're in your corner. And that counts for a lot.

In my mind's eye
Of course I realized that my parents and foster father couldn't be there, because they are dead. Nevertheless, I thought that being dead was about the worst possible excuse not to be present for this big day. So I decided that my parents and foster dad would definitely be there. When I was backstage, waiting to be announced, I envisioned them standing tall in the auditorium.

On the top left, top middle and top right in the audience. Fortunately, my foster mother was in the audience front row, alive and well. Everyone who was supposed to be there, was there. Because they should be.

Harry

As millions of people have, I've read the story of Harry Potter, the young orphan and wizard who learns how to perform magic (if you haven't, go on, read the story. It's amazing. I'll try not to reveal too much about the ending of that story, because it's just too brilliant not to experience it for yourself). The headmaster of Harry's school, Professor Dumbledore, appeared in a vision in Harry's mind, just before Harry had to face his sworn enemy, Lord Voldemort. Harry was given a Resurrection Stone by his Professor. The Resurrection Stone temporarily brings back the spirits of your lost loved ones, so you can communicate with them. Harry received this stone to use at the moment he needed courage and support the most. At the moment that Harry had to sacrifice himself for the greater good, this Resurrection Stone brought him a vision of his dead parents (and godfather) standing before him. His parents, who had died when Harry was just a baby. Harry asked them why they were there at that moment, after all this time. His mother peacefully replied with words that always bring me to tears: "We never left."

Harry's enemy, the evil Lord Voldemort, attacked Harry and almost killed him, when Harry had a vision of his Professor. He told Harry that he had a choice: to confront his enemy once more and put an end to this battle, or to 'go on'. Harry asked Dumbledore: "Is this real, or is it all just happening in my head?"

Dumbledore: "Of course it's happening in your head, Harry, but why should that mean it's not real?" Take a moment to feel the infinite power and love of these two sentences.

"We never left."

"Of course it's happening in your head, Harry, but why should that mean it's not real?"

Anyone who knows me and/or has read my first book 'So, You're An Orphan Now', can probably imagine why these words have been vitally important in preparing for my performance at TEDxDelft. Because it was exactly like that for me. I needed my parents to be there. And although envisioning them in the auditorium 'only' happened in my head, it was real to me and it worked like a charm. Because at that moment I felt connected to them. I believed that they had never left me, even if it was only in my heart. And I believe that one's heart is the most sacred place to keep the people you love and have to live without for the rest of your life.

I wanted the comfort of having this picture in my head: my lost loved ones in the packed room I was performing in. Because the story was about them and me, and I wanted them there with me. I would have given the world for them to be in the audience, chatting to one another and enjoying the whole day. The thing is, if they hadn't died, I wouldn't have been asked to be on that stage, speaking about how people can help children who are trying to build a better life for themselves without their parents. That was the cold truth.

Envisioning my parents and foster father in the audience supported me enormously. I felt that I would be able to deal with whatever crossed my path during my performance. Unfortunately, that was quite necessary. I'll tell you more about that in the next chapter, "It Ain't Over 'Til It's Over".

Joking about fear
Jerry Seinfeld, the stand-up comedian, once told this joke: "According to most studies, people's number one fear is public speaking. Number two is death. Does that seem right? That means to the average person, if you have to go to a funeral, you're better off in the casket than doing the eulogy."

Of course, this is just a joke. As Chad Schultz wrote in a blog post about this: "What do we mean when we say that people fear public speaking "more" than death? That given the choice, people would rather be put to death than give a speech? That seems unlikely." Think about it. Imagine this guy tapping you on the shoulder, saying: "Hey you. Either I will kill you right here and now, or you get up on that stage and talk to the lot of us."

Schultz states in his blog post that Seinfeld's joke was probably based on the 1977 Book of Lists. In this book, 'The 14 Worst Human Fears' are scored. A team of market researchers asked 3,000 U.S. inhabitants the question "What are you most afraid of?" Their answers are scored in percentages in this list:

1 Speaking before a group 41%
2 Heights 32%
3 Insects and bugs 22%
4 Financial Problems 22%
5 Deep water 22%
6 Sickness 19%
7 Death 19%
8 Flying 18%
9 Loneliness 14%
10 Dogs 11%
11 Driving/riding in a car 9%
12 Darkness 8%
13 Elevators 8%
14 Escalators 5%

However, this list of people's basic fears is almost forty years old. Did you notice that fear of death isn't even at the top of this list? Probably because people are thinking more often about daily scary things and tasks. Death is the end point after all, so no reason to fret over it today, unless you are really, really ill. Either way, you can't do anything about it. But you can do something about fear of speaking. If I followed Schultz' line of thinking, I know what I'd choose. Nevertheless, it's a funny joke by Seinfeld. Sometime's you shouldn't over-analyze things.

Now let's take a look at what most people are afraid of when we focus on just public speaking. Their biggest fears about speaking are: looking like a fool; boring the audience; being lost for words; people noticing your nervousness; people hating the presentation or, worse, getting up to leave while you're still giving it your best.

What was the fear about?

My stage anxiety wasn't about being afraid of not being able to manage my grief about having lost my parents. It was about having to manage my emotions about having lost my foster father, two months before my TEDx performance. My foster father, the main character in my talk, had died of asbestos cancer on December 3rd 2014. I strongly felt that if I were to burst into tears on stage, it would be counterproductive in terms of getting my empowering message across, my message designed to trigger the audience to change something for the struggling kids around them. For this reason, it was absolutely crucial that these emotions would not get tangled up on stage. Otherwise people in the audience might think "that's a courageous thing to do, sharing that personal story." But that wasn't my goal at all. My talk wasn't about me being brave. My talk was about people feeling empowered and encouraged to help today's kids, so they could get a better shot at life. Crying wasn't a constructive part of that equation.

The Switch Method

I dealt with my fear by using The Switch method. That's what I called it anyway. The university auditorium that would be the TEDx venue was adjacent to the cemetery where we had laid my foster dad to rest. Making the switch meant that in the weeks prior to my performance, I would visit the cemetery, then rehearse on stage and then return to the cemetery once more. I switched back and forth, in order to normalize the location in relation to my emotions.

The janitors at the TEDx venue were extremely helpful. They were gracious enough to allow me to practice my talk in the auditorium three times, at times that nobody was using the stage. That was a generous offer that I gratefully accepted. I took my video camera and tripod with me for every rehearsal to record my performance on stage. The first time, it was still an unsettling experience. The second time, I decided to jump rope on stage and make funny faces and do silly walks before recording the rehearsal. It made me feel more comfortable, as if this were my playground. And while I hadn't completely memorized my script by then, I still felt better and more confident.

My goal was to normalize the environment emotionally as much as I could, to experience the stage and the adjacent cemetery as if they were my livingroom. This method also worked because there was absolutely nobody in the room but me. I had been granted the privacy to go through the process. In my mind's eye, I could fill up the room any way I wanted to. And while rehearsing my talk, by reading small cards with key words that I laid out on the stage floor, I not only felt determined, but also increasingly confident. This proved to be a most effective strategy.

The third time I rehearsed on that stage, I got the jitters once again. I felt determined, but my speaker coaches had shared their concerns about my being overtrained and a bit obsessed with this particular performance. And they were right. They advised me to leave my script for approximately two weeks, and to start doing other things to increase my energy level. That was a tough decision I had to make. But I did it. And it was without a shadow of a doubt the right call.

After ten days of not reheasing or peeking at my script, I presented for the TEDx commission once more. The words rolled out of my mouth and heart with ease. They said to me: you are done rehearsing. Pick it up two days before TEDxDelft, and you'll be fine. This was a welcome confirmation.

After the reheasal, my speaker coaches also stated in unison that they thought I was way too caught up in the process. I heard and respected what they said. However, this way of preparing felt good to me, so I followed my own course. I have no regrets.

For many presenters, male and female, it's tempting (and for some even standard procedure) to switch to a testosterone level that's beyond Chuck Norris'. While oozing thoughts of invincibility they strike a Wonder Woman Power Pose. Not that I have anything against the Wonder Woman Power Pose. Frankly, I love Wonder Woman. And her power pose. It's helpful.

Science has proved that power poses do help you get through challenging moments more successfully. TED speaker Amy Cuddy shared enlightening insights and tips on performing.

Cuddy states that certain 'power poses' don't just change how others perceive you, but they also immediately change your body chemistry and therefore have a huge impact on how you are performing. And these body chemistry changes affect the way you do your job and interact with other people.

But however helpful they are, you don't need them to be able to perform. To be more precise: you can perform successfully without any power pose. But they might come in handy. Let's look at the following three powerful speakers.

President John F. Kennedy
Did JFK have a Power Pose? I don't know and I don't have the opportunity to ask the man. Was he charismatic? Absolutely. Was he able to connect to specific audiences? Definitely ("Ich bin ein Berliner!"). I don't know whether or not he had a Power Pose, but my guess is he didn't need one. Probably because he was the one that people wanted to impress, since he sat on the most powerful chair in the world. But John F. Kennedy wasn't born a President. He was privileged, talented, reasonably easy on the eyes, well-connected, smart and politically savvy. And had had lots of opportunities to practice.

Marianne Williamson
This woman embodies wisdom, perseverance and grace. In her book "A Return To Love" (1992), she used powerful words (commonly mis-attributed to Nelson Mandela's inauguration speech in 1994) that empower anyone who hears them.

"...Our deepest fear is not that we are inadequate.
Our deepest fear is that we are powerful beyond measure.
It is our light, not our darkness that most frightens us.
We ask ourselves, Who am I to be brilliant, gorgeous, talented, fabulous?
Actually, who are you not to be?
You are a child of God.
Your playing small does not serve the world.
There is nothing enlightened about shrinking so that other people won't

feel insecure around you.
We are all meant to shine, as children do.
We were born to make manifest the glory of God that is within us.
It's not just in some of us; it's in everyone.
And as we let our own light shine, we unconsciously give other people permission to do the same.
As we are liberated from our own fear, our presence automatically liberates others."

In Marianne's speeches, she shares her insights with great conviction, without losing her own personality for one second. She presents in an appealing way. You want to grasp every word. Furthermore, the content of what she shared in the speech fragment above stresses the importance of expressing oneself. Who needs a power pose when you have these words?

President Theodore D. Roosevelt

To this day, Roosevelt's brilliant and powerful words resonate in the minds of millions. TED and TEDx speaker Brené Brown chose a fragment of one of Roosevelt's speeches as one of her book titles: 'Daring Greatly'. I can recommend Brown's book, it's very powerful and useful for anyone who is expanding their comfort zone in order to excel in what Brown calls 'the arena'. Roosevelt wrote these words for his speech 'Citizenship In A Republic' at the Sorbonne in Paris, France. The following fragment resonated with Brene Brown so profoundly that she titled her book after it:

"It is not the critic who counts; not the man who points out how the strong man stumbles, or where the doer of deeds could have done them better. The credit belongs to the man who is actually in the arena, whose face is marred by dust and sweat and blood; who strives valiantly; who errs, who comes short again and again, because there is no effort without error and shortcoming; but who does actually strive to do the deeds; who knows great enthusiasms, the great devotions; who spends himself in a worthy cause; who at the best knows in the end the triumph of high achievement, and who at the worst, if he fails, at least fails while daring greatly, so that his place shall never be with those cold and timid souls who neither know victory nor defeat."

Roosevelt's words illustrate perfectly on their own that he was able to share his insights before a large crowd. They express strength through being vulnerable. And that is exactly what you need when you're sharing a message worth spreading. You need the guts to do this. Not necessarily by tapping into your resources of grit, but rather by carrying your words through the medium of your presence.

When Brené Brown chose the title 'Daring Greatly', she showed us that Roosevelt's words can still change people's lives today and tomorrow, all over the world. I'm not sure whether or not Roosevelt was practicing his Superman Pose in front of his bedroom mirror.

Maybe John, Marianne and Franklin all used the Superman or Wonder Woman Power Pose. Maybe they didn't. Either way, you are human just like them and rather than trying to rise above yourself like King Kong roaring from the top of the Empire State Building, it usually helps you more if you consider dropping your guard a little, and revealing a part of who you truly are and what you can bring to the table. Vulnerability takes a lot of courage. And it's worth your effort, I promise you.

Vulnerability in leadership
In a conversation I had with Dutch television personality Jet Sol, we shared which presentations stuck with us and made the biggest impression on us. Jet told me that one of the most powerful speech openings she ever heard was given by a corporate CEO (struggling with stage fright at the time), who said: "Good afternoon everybody. I'm used to leading this company, and I think I do it rather well. I'm used to sitting in the boardroom, watching you shiver while giving presentations in front of my desk. But truth be told, I'm very nervous about standing in front of you now. Giving a presentation takes courage. And it's not my forte. My sincere compliments for all you people who do it so well. So please bear with me, I'm doing the best I can. Okay, here we go, the annual financial statement."

This speech opening is sheer power. Vulnerability in action. This man knew his strengths and weaknesses, and used his weakness to rise above himself. At no point did he lose his dignity.

He understood very well that he was the one calling the shots in his company. And he knew that what he was going to say in his presentation would have the effect he was aiming for. Despite this fact he shared his emotions with his employees. This demands respect, and it builds an emotional bond with people.

Royal Jitters
If you are struggling a bit with stage fright or pre-event jitters, then you're in good company. Experts estimate that about seventy-five percent of the population (that's a lot!) has some level of anxiety about public speaking.

During my Christmas break in 2015, I was watching a BBC documentary about Elizabeth II, Queen of the United Kingdom, Canada, Australia and New Zealand, and Head of the Commonwealth. It was interesting to see how the production was prepared for addressing the public on camera for the first ever televised Christmas Broadcast in 1957. The Queen had performed brilliantly. Twenty-five years before, King George V had addressed the country via the 'wireless' (radio).

The Royal Family is experienced in how to express themselves and to address the public. It was refreshing to learn that Catherine, Duchess of Cambridge had publicly admitted that she's not too comfortable when speaking in public. She decided to get over it to deliver an address on children's mental health. If you watch the performance closely, you might recognize some signs of discomfort. But the fact that she did perform and did it so well, is what counts most.

Surprising Secret
Caroline Goyder's talk 'The Surprising Secret To Speaking With Confidence' at TEDxBrixton focuses on three strategies to feel more confident while performing. Caroline teaches three lessons. The first one: Practice your voice, for it is your most amazing instrument. And the simplest way to practice your voice, is to sing.

Caroline's second lesson is to learn how to carry yourself. When you pay attention, the most relaxed person in the room is usually the one with the most relaxed breath. They have control over their breath. Actors know this and use this knowledge every day. Your diaphragm is the key to regulating your system, it's how you calm yourself down. This provides you with confidence.

The third lesson Caroline teaches in her talk, is something that was applicable to my preparation for the eulogy at my foster dad's funeral, two months before my performance at TEDxDelft. Caroline stated that 'we breathe our thoughts': "All speach is outbreath. All song is outbreath. And all inbreath is thought. (...) You can control your voice by the idea of 'breath is thought'."
Caroline also referred to the ancient Romans, who understood that we breathe our thoughts. "The words 'inspiration' and 'respiration' have the same root. (...) And because we speak on the outbreath, all you have to think about, in the inbreath. And do you know the simplest way to think about the inbreath? Close your mouth. So who would have thought that the big secret I promised you, was that if you want confidence in speech, all you have to do is know when to shut your mouth." Powerful, isn't it?

In Case Everything Goes Terribly Wrong
Despite all your efforts, there are no guarantees that your performance will go as smoothly as you hope. You can prepare the best you can, but sometimes you just have bad luck. It can happen to all of us, whether new performer or seasoned entertainer.

During the Grammy ceremony on February 15th 2016, best-selling singer and icon Adele encountered a severe case of bad luck. There were technical difficulties that made the sound arrangements fail, and one of the microphones fell on top of a piano. Seconds after having started her song, Adele instantly noticed that there was something wrong, and she had to make a quick decision: go on or stop. She decided to go on. Moments later, she regretted that decision. A few days later, Adele was invited to the Ellen Show with Ellen Degeneres, to talk about her new album. But also about what had happened at the Grammy's.

Ellen asked Adele: "First of all, I understand that because you're so amazing and you're in front of all those people all the time, that it doesn't make you nervous. That you don't get stage fright. Or you still do?"

Adele ansered candidly: "More than ever, yeah."
Ellen was a bit surprised. "More than in the beginning? Because you feel more pressure because everyone just adores you and thinks "Oh my God, it's Adele, and you feel pressure, or..?"

Adele: "The more successful I get the more pressure there is. The further the fall."

Ellen: "When you start out, nobody really knows you."
Adele then reflects on what had happened at the Grammy's: "I don't think I can get that much worse than with the Grammy's, so I feel like I'm allright now. I dust it off. Because it was live television, I couldn't bust a joke and make the disaster my own. Next time I have any sound issues, I will stop. I'll say: Is there time to do it again? Or else: bye!"

Ellen understood and ended the conversation with a joke: "I hope it happens!"

Mental and physical preparation to feel more secure
Adele dealt with the situation the best way she thought fit, thought about it later, and decided to be prepared for the next time any unfortunate technical difficulties might occur. This is a very healthy way of dealing with hardship and disappointment. She later posted on Twitter: "Shit happens." And that basically covers it. Dust it off and go on.

My advice: learn from Adele's pain and think about how you want to deal with these kinds of hiccups. I believe in having a back-up plan. Not because you should be afraid that horror scenarios will become your perpetual fate, but to increase your feeling of security. Whatever may emerge, you will be able to deal with it. Just don't fret over all the horrible things that may happen. Think of a way of dealing with them and then let it go.

There is no need to replay any kind of negative fail tape in your mind. Envision the desired outcome and have faith you can do this because you are prepared.

You can do some practical things to feel at your best on the day of your performance. Your physical preparation is very important. Make sure that you get enough sleep. You need enough energy to cope with any jitters, to remain focused, and to perform in a dynamic and spirited way.

Start your day in a relaxed manner. Move around a bit, jump rope or do some other form of light exercise. I wake up every morning with at least ten minutes of meditation with the Headspace app on my iPhone (www.headspace.com). It helps me focus, helps me to get anchored and relaxed and also to feel more energetic. Meditation helps you to become more mindful of your thoughts by focusing on your breathing.

If you're haunted by feelings and thoughts of stage fright and feel the symptoms of this sensation rushing through your body, meditation provides a sense of calmness and clarity to help you become free to be yourself on stage. Remain open to this outcome.

Food and hydration

Make sure to hydrate yourself during the day. Don't drink too much water right before going on stage, for obvious reasons. Do not skip meals, even if you feel too nervous to eat anything. Take light meals that you are familiar with and that are high in protein, just like athletes do. Rather than fat cheese or peanut butter, choose cottage cheese or eggs and combine them with any kind of carbohydrates. This prevents low blood sugar, dizziness, fatigue and indecisiveness (really). Avoid sugar crashes (try to stay away from candy with high sugar levels) and too much caffeine. This was something I also researched before my talk.

I looked up nutritional advice for athletes in 'Nancy Clark's Sports Nutrition' (1997, publisher: Human Kinetics). I knew a thing or two about nutrition because I have been active as a recreational speed skater on ice for years. I felt I needed to adjust my knowledge for this particular event, and the book proved itself to be very useful. Clark advises in her book to take into account at what time you will be performing. As a guideline she advises:

> 10AM event: Eat a high carbohydrate dinner the evening before, with extra water. Have your breakfast by 7AM and eat something you usually take for breakfast.
>
> 2PM event: Eat a high carbohydrate breakfast and a light

lunch. Or combine them in a brunch by 10AM. Drink extra water up to noon.

8PM event: Eat a high-carbohydrate breakfast and lunch and have a light dinner by 5PM. Drink extra fluids all day, but be careful with that the last ninety minutes before your performance.

All day event: Two days before the event, cut back exercise to rest the body, rest completely the day before, eat a high carbohydrate breakfast, lunch and dinner the day before and drink extra fluids, eat a high carbohydrate breakfast that you can tolerate on the day of the event, and snack every ninety minutes to two hours on carbohydrates during the day if possible, eat lunch if you can. This will keep your energy flowing throughout the day. Drink water before you get thirsty.

Once I made the mistake of joining an event crew for dinner. This was not a good idea because there were dishes on the menu that I knew my body didn't tolerate very well. At that time, I didn't want to offend anyone who had made the arrangements. I would advise you to choose (or prepare and bring along) whatever meal you feel comfortable with. Ignoring your own needs because you want to please everyone is not a good strategy. You can't please everyone. The most important thing is that you perform well. Anyone having your best interests at heart who is also working towards a successful event will not stand in your way.

Develop a pre-event routine
Many athletes have their own routines prior to their performance. These routines vary from a few preparation exercises to an array of rituals. While these rituals may help them in getting ready, they might also be a weak spot. If one of the rituals isn't possible for any reason, this may endanger his or her chances of being successful. This depends on the complexity of the ritual. If it's just a short prayer or a simple oddity such as clapping your hands twice, there's no problem. But if your personal ritual involves howling at a full moon, while running barefoot on a freshly mowed lawn,

things might get complicated.

Pre-event routines however are useful. At TEDxDelft, we threw a ball at each other very fast. This worked well. It distracted speakers from the sharp edes of their nerves and synchronized the very active brain with body movements. It made us get focused and sharp in a matter of seconds.

I also had a music playlist to prepare myself before rehearsals and the actual event. 'Believe In Yourself' by Lena Horne often was on shuffle play. Other songs that made me feel good were 'Working On A Dream' (Bruce Springsteen), 'This Woman's Work' and 'Breathing' (Kate Bush), 'Engel' (Rammstein), 'Just Say Yes' (Snow Patrol) and 'Cantaloop' (US3). Music really does help.

Emotion Management Tip From A Celebrity
In a Dutch television show called College Tour, famous people are being interviewed by a journalist with a live audience of students. The students get the opportunity to ask the celebrity some questions. One of the episodes was an interview with Sting. One student asked Sting how he usually deals with situations in which he has to perform on stage, feeling deep emotions while singing a particular song that means a great deal to him. Sting answered with some excellent practical tips.

The first tip he shared: "I visualize a glass wall between me and the audience. Not to create more distance, but to let my emotions bounce back to me, and leave them be with their own emotions."

The second tip Sting shared was: "It's important for the audience to feel connected to you, even at moments you feel you might get overwhelmed. In order to create the connection within your safety zone, I look at the audience at eye level, but I'm not making eye contact. Nobody notices that. I just look at a spot in between people."

He adds one more tip to cope with emotion during concerts: "At times I feel I could get choked up while singing, I avoid looking at the audience, but I make visualize the words I have to sing just above the audience. I then let the words do the work: I sing them the best I can, while disconnecting my own emotions. I trust the words and their power; if they move people, they just need a little bit of me."

Sting's three tips have helped me when I presented my first book. My foster dad was in the audience, and I spoke about the wonderful things he had done for me when I was just a teenager. It wouldn't have been a shameful thing if I would have cried on stage. But I didn't want to. I felt that crying wouldn't add anything to the event. And I wanted it to be a joyous day. That book presentation was definitely one of the best days of my life.

Grit & Guts: macho behaviour or true courage
You don't have to boast, but you have to stand your ground. Find your balance in this. From time to time, I meet speakers who have customized certain behaviours, that differ from their natural behaviour. I usually wonder if they know that this is a rather transparent facade. Seeing through this kind of behaviour can be amusing. The image of a pufferfish pops into my mind whenever I see someone boast beyond normal proportions.

Charisma
When you ask ten people to descibe the word 'charisma', chances are you get ten different answers. If you look up definitions in the dictionary, charisma is descibed as "a special personal quality or power of an individual making him or her capable of influencing or inspiring large numbers of people". Another description is "a quality inherent in a thing which inspires great enthusiasm and devotion." Some people are perceived as being charismatic, while others have to work on it. Some will never be perceived as such. In case this turns out to be you unfortunate fate, there is also good news: there is always your skill set.

That last terrifying moment before taking the plunge
There is something odd and special about the last moment of fear before you do something that you've been preparing for. At that exact moment, all kinds of contradictory thoughts may battle inside your head and body. "This is a huge mistake! I can't do this! My talk sucks! I didn't know it before, but you see, I'm a fraud! Can I just go home? Oh my, I'm going to publicly humiliate

myself! What was I thinking! I'm going to throw up. I will never agree to present again. Who asked me to do this? I will kill them! Get me out of here...maybe a fire might chase everyone out of the room..."

The best thing about having gone through this once, is that you recognize it the next time it happens. And then you can see it for what it really is: it's the moment just before something wonderful and great is about to happen. You are stretching your comfortable boundaries far beyond anything you have ever done before, and you are exploring all the other things you might be capable of doing. That's an amazing thing. This is by far the most important moment to notice. And it's also the exact moment that someone dear to you should calm you down. Because it might not feel great, going though this anguish: you're amygdala (the part of your brain that processes emotions, survival instincts, and memory) is working extra hours and adrenalin is pumping through your body like some sort of toxic espresso on an empty stomach in the middle of the night. The good news is: your amygdala stops sending alarm signs to your body around ninety seconds after first kicking in. So you can just wait it out for a minute and a half. Focusing on your breathing usually is the best method to deal with the sharp edge of panic.

A smartphone app such as Headspace might help you to refocus on your breathing and to channel your emotions and stress levels.

At my moment of sheer terror, I called my director Ric. I needed to call him on the phone, because he couldn't be back stage since he was not one of the official TEDx appointed speaker coaches. I had asked him to help me during my rehearsal weeks. My official speaker coaches were instructed not to help me or any of the other speakers on the day of the TEDx conference. This struck me as odd and unreasonable, but this was the explicit demand of the stage manager. She wanted control of the production and asked all speaker coaches to stop coaching after the final rehearsal the night before the conference. The speaker coaches obliged, but I had my doubts about this agreement. I needed someone to be there for me. So I picked up the phone and called Ric. And it worked.

BEFORE

Lorde @lorde Feb 25

Such an honour getting to perform #BRITs2016 paying tribute to my hero.

AFTER

Lorde @lorde Feb 25

I was so nervous in the wings,

and then I whispered to myself

"just sing it to David",

and nothing else mattered.

3,375 retweets 14,132 likes

—@Lorde on Twitter
about her tribute to David Bowie
at the Brit Awards 2016

INTERVIEW

Ric Berretty:

"Everyone who truly wants to perform, is able to."

Ric Berretty is an experience designer, actor and director. Ric has been active in theatre since high school, as an actor as well as a director. He has travelled the world with Up With People, *an international group of 110 theatre enthusiasts. Since 2002, Ric is a paid director and actor and has worked in many productions.*

Ric, I asked you to help me prepare my performance at TEDxDelft. And I am very grateful for your help, for you have taught me many things. For instance, learning long scripts. What is your own process in this?
One of the strategies that worked well for you, is something I do myself as well, when learning large theatre scripts. It's telling the whole story in about two minutes, so you integrate the entire story arc so you won't forget it. This is helpful in case you forget where you were in the story when you're on stage. Just taking two seconds to fly through that story arc gets you back on track. That's the best way to prepare yourself and to prevent disappointing moments. Training this story arc swiftly gives you feeling for the whole narrative. That's what you're learning in essence: a narrative. Not the script. If you forget a word, it won't be the end of the world.

The key in learning a script, is that you're not really learning a script! During the first phase of preparing, you're getting to know your story, through and through. You do this by creating associations. You search for cause-effect in the story. This is the best way for people to follow your story and for you to learn every aspect of it. You do this by creating stops in your story, let's call them stepping stones. Little game changers, needed to bring the story and the experience of the story.

In the second phase of your preparation, you have already created a solid base. Not just in the core of the story, because you'd already written that. You work on a base of posture, tone of voice, stage presence and an overall basis, physically, vocally and mentally. You have to create a basis of relaxation, concentration, imagination and observation. The beauty of this is that you're bringing the story from this basis, you are triggering your physical memory. This helps your brain to internalize your story and your performance.

What methods did you use while helping me prepare for my talk?
The first challenge was to chop the story up in crunchy bites. We did that by writing keywords on small cards. We started out with forty cards. Then, we reduced the number of cards to twenty-five, fifteen and ultimately, we worked with ten cards with one keyword on each of the cards.

We also worked with the principle of 'the power of three'. The activating message in your talk was that the audience should learn to (1) notice children who have to live without their parents; (2) facilitate them with a short-term solution; and (3) empower these children to build a better life for themselves. Notice. Facilitate. Empower. The power of three just helps. Think of concepts such as 'reuse, reduce, recycle' and 'Huey, Dewey and Louis'.

We used the power of pausing. Not just in your performance, but also in between rehearsals. We call this 'incubation'. Your brains are doing part of the work for you while you're taking a break. It's like writing a final thesis for a college graduation; while you're washing dishes, showering or cleaning the house, your brain is structuring and filtering what you've been working on.

By introducing your talk with the metaphor of walking a tight rope, you added confrontation and a little bit of humour, which painted a picture for your audience. The metaphor reeled your audience in. At the end, you came back to the metaphor and the story came full circle. This hyperbole is mentally pleasing for the audience, and it helps them accept the practical advice that you want them to integrate in their behaviour. An important part of your preparation was about audience participation. We knew in advance that there would be limited possibility for interacting with the audience, since it would be a TEDx setting. We decided to instruct the audience to do something for a few seconds, while you created a moment of silence, the "Now, think silently for yourself..." part of your talk. This made it possible to let the audience do something while integrating your message, while establishing a stronger connection with the whole audience.

At TEDx, it is important to have a 'script' to keep oversight over the whole thing. But by all means, give yourself space and permission to choose synonyms if you need them on stage. These strategies can help you achieve this.

Ric, could you tell a bit more about your relationship with narrative?
Narrative is crucial to me. I know exactly where and when I'm on stage and in the story, also in relation to all other actors on stage. When I feel secure about that factor, I know everything will be fine. I'll know what to say and the right moment, and sometimes, if I'm in a piece where there is a little room for improvisation, I may choose different words from time to time. The next logical step is to know every single line. Acting in a theatre piece differs from TEDx. One of the tools I use for learning my lines, is the iOS app Line Learner. I also advised you to use that, which you did. Good for you!

Can you tell a bit more about how we translated my emotions to creating a performance?
Telling an emotional story with an educational goal is always a necessary challenge. This process isn't about disconnecting emotion, but to translate it to the stage in a way that it helps the audience in adopting your message and to change their future behaviour. This is also what we're doing in the theatre every day.

In rehearsals, we explore everything and some sentiments and nerve ends may be painfully exposed, but once you find the right way to deal with them, the acting starts. This process prevents our emotions from overwhelming actors and performers.

Have you experienced differences in learning processes with the actors in your plays?
Every person has a different way of learning and internalizing things. There are people who learn at the mise-en-scène, and people who are open to the learnings at an earlier stage. And some actors learn their lines best in relation to other actor's roles. This might be challenging in case the other actor forgets his lines. One shouldn't be solely dependent on other people's lines. And then there's the type of actor who is very able to learn huge amounts of script, but get to know the emotional and real meaning of the contents of them.

Would you like to share about preparing performances?
I always think from the perspective of the receiver, in this case: the audience. How does the piece land with them? What do they see first? And then? How do I address them? If I have to make a choice between what's comfortable for the performing actor or for the audience, I always choose the audience. They are always my first priority.

What's been the most challenging production you have directed?
Surely, this would be 'Murder in the Nativity Set', because we had 10 actors, 35 parts to play, 3 sets, 25 under aged ballerinas, 3 camels, puppetry, singing, dancing, magic tricks and a snow ball fight including the audience. It was a delight to direct, and a bizarre combination of humour, story, timing, treating the audience and heaps of fun. But it was very, very challenging indeed.

Have you ever experienced stage fright?
Every time, excruciatingly so. Fortunately, this melts away at the sight of the audience. That won't ever change for me. I deal with it differently than I did years ago; though: I take my time before

every performance, to experience every aspect of the play in my head. Mentally, script wise, emotionally, the narrative, the whole package. Taking my time keeps me focused and provides me with the confidence I need until the moment I see the audience.

How do you deal with coaching performers or actors who aren't as extroverted as you are?
Extroversion has nothing to do with it. Some people have to be encouraged a bit more, and others have to be slowed down. To me, extroversion and introversion are irrelevant. Directing actors is an empathetic process to me. I stand next to them, and guide them through their process. That process comprises directing people so they will give the production their best. And as a director, you have to know where you're going with the project.

Do you have a specific strategy to deal with actor's jitters just before curtain call?
I remind people of the agreements we made before the performance, and confirm that they are ready. That they can make it happen, that there's no reason why they shouldn't be able to. And that if things may go differently than they anticipated, they may still make it work because they have enough bases. I remind them of the fact that they have become the story. It's not just a lesson they've learned. That's the difference. When you have internalised the part, you're ready to share it with the audience.

Have you ever encountered a lost cause?
In case of giving a presentation: everyone that really wants to be helped, can be helped. And 'lost cause' is not a particularly pleasant description. Some people lack the motivation to go for it. In that case, there is nothing I can do. But anyone who wants to make it work, can do it.

"This is my story.
I don't care what
the circumstances are.
These next eighteen
minutes are mine."

SHOWTIME

Two Black Screens

In a perfect world, everything goes as planned.

When Sylvia, the TEDxDelft speakers liaison, had courteously introduced me, I walked past the big red letters T, E and D and the slightly smaller X on the stage. The crew had carefully painted the letters, so that the stage would look as professional as possible.

In front of the main stage, a smaller, triangular shaped stage had been built. That triangle was my spot. Two monitors had been attached to this stage for my personal visual aids: the digital clock, counting back to zero, and the slide deck that would also appear behind me on the big screen.

Both monitors were black. And nothing happened. Initially, I got angry. The first thought that popped into my head was: "If this is the way you want to play it, bring it on. This is my room and this is my story. I don't care what the circumstances are. These next eighteen minutes are mine." I wasn't directing my anger towards anyone in particular, even though I felt that I had every right and reason to be angry with the person responsible for not providing my monitors with the correct information.

I wasn't planning on using a slide deck until two weeks prior to the conference, because I felt that I could carry the story without visual support. I still believe that to be true. I had however agreed to create slides, because the TEDxDelft stage manager wanted the talks be visually more appealing than just a woman standing on stage, speaking. So I obliged. I hadn't thought that this would pose a problem, since I had told the organization that I wasn't going to hold a laser pointer in my hands to flick through the slides. I was already holding a card as a prop, and I wanted to have at least one hand completely free during my performance.

But I did need the clock, ticking back to zero. Or did I?

The feeling of panic-filled insecurity had disappeared in a blink of an eye, and was replaced by a shot of anger and then fierce, focused determination. "Be brave", I told myself. I breathed in, and started my first sentence.

"On Valentine's Day 1990, I received my first Valentine's Card."

This was my stage. And my parents were in the room, for they were in my heart.

"I was fourteen years of age, and this is the card."

I took the card out of my dress pocket and showed it to the audience, which felt at that moment like holding a window to my past. I hadn't thought of the card like that before, but I had chosen it to use it as a prop. The window metaphor presented itself for the first time in my mind at that moment, even though I had rehearsed the words so often. The creation of something new is never over until you've completed the entire performance.

The monitors were still black. I decided to ignore them, ignore any setbacks and just go with what I had rehearsed for months. And I hoped I'd still be in the eighteen minutes time limit.

I read the contents of the Valentine's card out loud, and shared what had happened the day after I had received it.

"On February 15th, my brave, beautiful and creative mother died of aggressive lung cancer."

To illustrate how it had felt for my sister and me to have to take care of ourselves after our mother and father had passed away, I used 'walking on a tight rope' as a metaphor, as a trigger to give the audience an opportunity to create an image in their minds, connected to my story.

After a minute or so, some people started laughing. I thought that was rather odd, since I had just shared a vulnerable experience in public. In a split second, I deduced that the reason for the hilarity was something that had nothing to do with me, but rather something on the big screen behind me on the stage. I paused for a second (so that the editors could cut that out in the definitive TEDx channel video on YouTube), turned my head and saw what was wrong. One of the big letters, the T, had toppled over. EDxDelft, the letters read on stage. I turned back to the audience, was silent for a second, and without even thinking about it, I smiled, and uttered: "So Mr. T is our first casualty. We're going to mourn him later. But first, the dead parents."

Silence.

I waited a second, and realised that I was the only one who had the liberty to tell a morbid joke about my story. And the room was mine once more.

I continued and I felt more grounded than ever before, despite the technical glitches that had happened around me. Actually, these proved themselves to be blessings in disguise, since they put me in a super-focused zone, in which I had the freedom to tap into one of my core qualities - improvisation - to save my talk and to connect with the audience. Improvisation. That was the one of the things that TEDx talks are not about. They're all about preparation. But I can tell you, if you're great at improvisation and circumstances that you have zero to no influence over are about to ruin your big moment, you bet your bottom dollar that you should use your core talent to save your performance. I felt powerful.

In the YouTube video, you can't see anything of the falling T incident because they've edited out the whole thing, as well as my joke. That was exactly what I was hoping for. After editing, the video was sixteen minutes and twenty-one seconds long. Rehearsing with a clock had paid off: in the end I hadn't needed oneon stage. Time was on my side. Thanks to a lot of rehearsing.

Up to the very last second of the talk, I felt at ease. I said "Thank you" and left the stage. The feeling of relief, pride and love was overwhelming.

The great thing about a TEDx audience is that everyone wants you to succeed. There is a snag: they also expect you to perform accordingly.

KEY TAKEAWAYS

Putting It All Together: It Ain't Over 'Til It's Over

Everyone Wants You To Succeed
The great thing about a TEDx audience is that everyone wants you to succeed. There is, however, a snag: they also expect you to perform accordingly. TEDx has set a high bar, and everyone knows that speakers take a lot of time and effort to prepare. You get a positive vibe from the audience, but you have to make it worth their while.

Just Do It Right The First Time
There are no retakes on stage at TEDx. This is something you just have to deal with. When my monitors blacked out, I couldn't stop presenting and say "Hey! Can anyone please fix the monitors? Thanks!" Not a chance. It would have ruined everything.

Do Not Fear Fear
There is no shame in having stage fright or having healthy pre-presentation jitters. Just don't let it take over your abilities. Often, we are suffering more because of our fears, that that we're rightfully afraid of something. Face your fears, learn to live with them, instead of battling against them. Don't deny your fears. Unleash your inner Pippi, Batman or other superhero.

If You Forget Where You Were In Your Talk
If you get a black-out during your talk, take a breath, and remember the stepping stones that your talk consists of. Just choose the one that's most clear to you, and pick it up from there.

Backstage
The backstage area of a TEDx conference can be a great place to connect and make new friends. You are all in this together and this creates a bond. This also be an intense stress zone where people are pacing and preparing in their own way for the challenge ahead.

When Speaker Coaches Stop Coaching

It has come to my attention that policies vary for speaker coaches during conferences. At the conference where I performed, all speaker coaches were instructed by the stage manager to stop coaching on the day of the event. This was a stressful rule for me, because I had a severe case of stage fright that day, for the first time in my life as a speaker. My speaker coaches weren't available to me that day.

Fortunately, I had the possibility to call Ric, my director, twenty minutes before going on stage. This made a tremendous difference for me. I strongly advise speaker coaches to assist speakers on the day of the event, if the speaker indicates he or she needs assistance.

The same goes for privacy on the day of the event. I was probably the only speaker who chose not to sit in the audience during other people's presentations. I watched their performances via the livestream from the Green Room and cheered for them there. I made this decision because I didn't want my focus to be disturbed by well-meaning friends and a boyfriend who wanted to connect with me. I have not apologized for this. You should do what you need to do on a day like that.

Sitting in the audience could also have triggered thoughts that wouldn't be helpful. Thoughts like "Oh my gosh, my friends are all waving at me and I'm so nervous!," or "That stage is so BIG, how on earth did I think I could do THIS?" All the other speakers were more courageous than I was: they were all in the audience the whole day. I admire that.

Core message here: do whatever works for YOU. You don't have to please anybody in any way besides performing well on stage. You're not there to be the host(ess).

Charging up

Truth be told, before the whole event started that day, I did connect with all of the speakers, and we coached each other through the last excruciating minutes before each talk, just before everyone left the Green Room for their own performance. The day before the actual event was completely filled with dress rehearsals (2 PM to 11 PM) and the speaker's dinner. A great way to connect to the team of amazing speakers, crew and tech team. The speakers were staying in a nearby hotel, which was extremely comfortable. Not only because of the comfortable bed and well-prepared breakfast, but also because I didn't have to get up at 3:40 and 5:15 am to comfort my elderly cat. I completely adored my cat. I did. I really, really did (unfortunately, he passed away nine months later). But the night before performing at a TEDx conference, you need your sleep. You need to charge up!

No Notes on Stage, Please
The TEDx organization prefers it when you learn your talk by heart. I agree with them, for if you have rehearsed well and you have internalised your story and you know everything there is to know about what you are going to say, you won't need a piece of paper. And I admit, whenever I see a performer use a printed copy, a thought like 'hasn't he rehearsed enough?' pops up.

Some performers at TED and TEDx conferences intentionally use notes on paper. Valid reasons for this are, for example, that someone may be verbally impaired, the speech is extremely long (President Obama reads The State of the Union from paper) or there are other relevant factors.

I feel that it's acceptable to use paper notes on stage, as long as it isn't a TEDx talk. Perhaps that's a bit judgmental of me. But I know how much work and dedication goes into preparing for a talk like this. And if I and many other people are willing to walk that extra mile, I expect others to do this as well. If you need paper notes because you didn't prepare well enough, I think you're not really ready to perform. If you need paper notes because of a valid reason, it's completely okay with me. There is a difference between being challenged in a particular way and just not giving it your best.

Recently, a series of TEDx talks by people from my own country was published on YouTube. When I watched one of them that I was particularly looking forward to, I noticed that the man on stage was sharing a powerful insight...by reading ninety-five percent of it from paper. I found it distracting. A few people asked him about it afterwards. He said that he had been nervous beforehand and on stage, that he needed something to hold on to, and that he had re-written his talk on numerous occasions during the weeks before the conference. I think there were two mistakes in his preparation, and one conclusion.

The first mistake in my opinion was, that he should have taken more time to rehearse what he had already written, so that he had internalised the organic story curve. He wouldn't have needed the notes because he would have known every stepping stone in his story.

The second mistake was that the speaker had re-written the last part of his speech over and over again. Even in the last week before the event, he was still editing. Any well-equipped speaker coach should have intervened and would have given him a choice between two options: 1.) go with what you already have and focus on feeling comfortable performing; 2.) re-write your talk and postpone your performance until the next edition of that particular TEDx event. There might be an exception to this second option: if there is enough time to re-write and rehearse so that you can perform confidently without peeking at your piece of paper.

When Reading From Paper Is Allowed
When Monica Lewinsky gave her TED talk 'The Price of Shame', she had a paper copy of her speech on the stage. This is one of the examples of speaking with a cheat sheet that I do not mind at all. While I noticed that she looked at the piece of paper from time to time, there was not one moment where I felt that she wasn't engaging with the audience. Her courageous and wholehearted talk about surviving public humiliation and deep shame resonated with many people in the audience, and with me.

When I listened to Monica's talk on YouTube, I realized that she wasn't just extremely brave because she shared the story about this intense part of her life, but also that every single person in the room had already associated her name with that phase of her life in vivid imagery, seventeen years before she was even standing on that stage. They had never forgotten her name. Furthermore, Lewinsky wanted to share more in her talk than just her experiences in overcoming shame and humiliation; she wanted to address cyber bullying and harrassment on social media, and the profound impact of this on peoples' lives, victims as well as their loved ones.

Lewinsky's TED talk struck me as being powerful and engaged. Her performance demonstrated courage by showing her vulnerability and grace under pressure, and she valiantly took up the challenge. Her talk was over twenty-two minutes, which is longer than the TED regulations aim for. Considering the widespread media and the audience's attention to the first part of Monica's story and the necessity to switch to her idea worth spreading, she needed some time. That is completely understandable. It can be quite challenging to build a bridge from a personal experience that so many people have fierce opinions about, to presenting a learning that the audience might integrate so other people can benefit from it. That's a big task, and Lewinsky succeeded in that mission.

I can also relate to her need to hold on to something on stage. When I spoke at my foster dad's funeral, I needed a piece of paper as well. Not because I had trouble memorizing what I wanted to share, but because it was excruciatingly hard to speak at such a grief-filled moment.

Timing, pace and imagination on stage

Perhaps you have seen J.J. Abrams' talk 'The Mystery Box' at TED. It is about discovering the mystery box in creative storytelling, and using any creative and technological means to visualize a story, and to engage people with that story. In terms of rehearsing and pace, some speaker coaches may think this talk is not a top notch performance. I however believe that his talk is just wonderful, magnetic and it keeps me on the edge of my seat. J.J. Abrams is a director, producer, writer, composer and storyteller and he uses his extremely creative palet of vivid expressions and verbal imagery to put his message in your mind and heart. This shouldn't come as a surprise, given the fact that he is the creator of many epic films and series such as Star Wars - The Force Awakens, Mission: Impossible III, Lost and more.

In his talk, sometimes he doesn't even finish sentences and

jumps on to something else. It's a creative mind in motion.

A classic approach to public speaking would condemn not finishing sentences, for it does create some mayhem in your mind. But in essence, that's also the beauty of it. For you need you own vivid mind to completely grab his message. And that's how he activates you. J.J. Abrams also uses visual aids in his presentation. He shows some clips from his films to explain how he made decisions about how to visualize certain storylines. The way he does this is absolutely endearing, in my opinion. When I see him share his story, he resembles a child in a candy store. He shows sheer joy in sharing this creative process. Not just because he wants the audience to get the best part of his message, but also because he is so enthusiastic about his projects that he allows himself to be sucked into the story once more.

I feel that one of the most attractive features of any human being is the ability to surrender oneself to something - a project, an experience, anything - in a way that any self-conscious layer is peeled off. If you can let that happen, creating a crack in the polished layer of professionalism, while still enticing people to engage in your story, if only in ther minds, to let your message land properly, then you are a true story maker.

There are several moments in his talk where he refers to his childhood, where the root of his creativity sprouted. Abrams shares how his grandfather provided all kinds of resources to create things. A synthesizer for creating music and atmospheres, for example. And a photo camera. These are valuable things to give to a young boy, and they provided him with the instruments to create imagery. He expresses his gratitude for the opportunities and resources that were available to him while growing up. There is absolutely no hint at any moment of sense of entitlement. Just gratitude, inspiration, imagination, expression and lots of joy in the creative process.

The one powerful prop Abrams uses is a mystery box that he had bought decades ago for fifteen dollars. He brought it with him on stage in a backpack. After showing the audience the box, he left it on stage on a little red desk for the entire presentation. I don't know whether or not he opened his back pack on stage on purpose, but to me this demonstrated the care with which he treats objects that matter a lot to him. He protects emotional keepsakes. And that also adds to his story. The box symbolizes the consecutive moments of mystery within a longer story, a film for instance.

Verbal mayhem, elation and lack of respect
There are however also completely different scenarios of presenters creating mayhem and taking their story all over the place, without achieving their goal (which is to bring a message across clearly and vividly). This usually results in the audience feeling increasingly awkward, up to a point where you feel the amount of shame you think the failing speaker should feel. In Dutch, we have an expression for this that translates into something like 'vicarious shame'.

Vicarious shame
The last time I felt vicarious shame rushing through my veins was when I attended a book presentation of one of my colleagues. He is a wonderful professional and had written a useful book on networking via LinkedIn. He had invited three speakers to share their insights on their own profession. Two of them were true professionals and maintained a comfortable balance between sharing information and engaging the audience. They remained on topic and were respectful of their given time limit. Their talks were easy to follow and entertaining, even for people who were reasonably new to the topic. These speakers treated everyone in the room respectfully and engaged with them in a positive, courteous manner. All in all, these were just good talks, well rehearsed and performed by experienced speakers.

The third speaker, however, wasn't as seasoned as his predecessors. He energetically climbed the stage and started talking about himself. About how he had just graduated and therefore had the most up-to-date knowledge in his professional field. And that he was ready to teach us all. He hadn't realised yet that graduating college is the first stepping stone on a very long journey that is called a career. Over fifty percent of the audience stared at him in bewilderment. The two speakers who had just been on stage exchanged looks. There was a short moment in which I felt compassion, because he was just starting out after graduating college and wanted to make a convincing statement on stage. I could relate to that feeling, because we all were beginners once. Confidence is a useful instrument. The first years of speaking professionally form a steep learning curve, and being in that process can feel exhilarating as well as humbling. I've felt that spectrum of emotions. Everybody has to start somewhere. The moment this young man started talking about networking with social media, it became clear that the vast majority of people in the room were already familiar with this. He only shared the basics of networking. His tone of voice was belittling and he used diminutives profusely. "So then you'll take this booklet and then you'll write some tweeties, and you jot in some hashtaggies, ya know what I mean? You should try it! If you practice it, you can learn this too, and get as successful as I am!" It was horrible. And that was not the end of it.

He continued with an announcement that he had started a challenge. "If you are grateful for my lesson today, you may ask me to speak at your business or event. Because I have made a bet with a friend of mine. I want to be on fifteen stages in the next five weeks. You can make that happen! So if you want to hire me, give me a call or ask me during the networking round."

There was silence. A long, awkward silence. A silence filled with disbelief at what had just happened. The speaker paused, with a hopeful and enthusiastic expression on his face that almost predicted jazz hand gestures. He bowed, and that was our cue to give him our applause. Which of course we did. Because that's what you do. It was one of those moments when you don't know exactly where to start in terms of giving feedback. This leads to not saying anything at all, which is also not a very good option, since you don't want this nice, well-meaning guy to go haywire in his next presentations. If he even gets booked. This event made me think of my aunt Jose's often used expression: "I don't talk about myself. You'll do that when I leave the room anyway." Jazz hands!

The Four Phases of Learning and Building Experience
This young man's situation can be fixed. He is (probably) not a lost cause. He was unconsciously incompetent. Which is not necessarily a bad thing in the beginning of your career, but is does require additional coaching. And probably a temporary break from performing in public.

The next phase in his development will undoubtedly be realizing that he is incompetent. He'll then know and fully understand what went wrong on stage. This is the most confrontational phase, because most people who are in this phase probably experience some amount of shame. Feeling shame is never pleasant. The beauty of it is that you can choose to feel compassion for yourself, if you are able to do that at this point. Some of us have learned to judge our own mistakes gently. A useful trait, because it provides you with the courage to sail through the shame and pick up the pieces and to start right at the level where you are, knowing that you'll have to learn much more. And that that can be a wonderful journey in itself. In this phase of discovering that you're not as competent as the more seasoned speakers, it's of vital importance not to keep on boasting, just to keep up your confidence level. I'm not saying that you should hide yourself, never enter the limelight again and slither into oblivion. I'm suggesting that extra training would be welcome, and to watch and learn more. To fill yourself up with inspiration. And to practice in safe environments.

In this process, the next step is to become consciously competent. A speaker now knows what he or she is able to do, and has built up a body of work and experiences. And gradually grows into the phase of being unconsciously competent, yet always open to soak up new tips and advice, in order to improve their own performance and abilities, without a grand finale in mind. Because speaking professionally can be a career in itself, and as a professional, you should always be searching for ways to learn more.

Gesturing and personal appearance
In most books on public speaking, there is usually advice on

personal appearance and gesturing. Some of the advice in these books is valuable, some of it is not.

Also, some experts tend to contradict one another about what's advisable and what isn't. One expert can tell you not to wear a piece of jewelry that distracts the audience's attention from the content of your speech, and another expert can advise you to wear something that will linger in your audience's memory.

Another example: one expert may emphasize the importance of always wearing formal clothing, even when you're asked to speak in an informal setting. Another expert may push you towards wearing statement clothing that nobody else wears, or a particular quirky tie or a longer beard and a fashionable pair of glasses. I trust that these experts all mean well. But in the end, dressing right for your public speaking engagement is always the sum of adjusting to the occasion while maintaining your own style and identity.

It's a fact that we as communicating human beings also speak with our bodies. Our body language reinforces or denies the things we say. Nonverbal communication provides us with enormous amounts of information about what a person is trying to say, and what s/he is trying to hide. Many books, blogs, YouTube videos and social media postings about public speaking and performance emphasize the importance of choosing the right gestures while presenting. Develop your own style!

Over-analyzing gestures

If you do a quick search on Google with the keywords 'public speaking gesture tips', you'll find a ginormous amount of information. I don't think I have to repeat all those tips in this book. Also because I think some speaking experts tend to go a bit overboard with their analysis and interpretations of nonverbal gesturing, and the communication strategies that speakers supposedly use. I must admit that I laughed when I read in TED and TEDx performer, shame researcher and entrepreneur Brené Brown's book Daring Greatly (I love that book and Brene's insights), that Brene was surprised to read an analysis about her physical gestures during her presentation. She comments in

Daring Greatly: "I'd certainly never used any conscious storytelling calculus in designing my talks. In fact, when I read the occasional analysis of my TED talks, I'm shocked to see how people take the smallest gestures, from glances to pauses, and use them to apply labels and formulas to my work. "At minute four, Brené shifts her body to the left and gives a slight half grin. This is known as the Soft Smile Pivot and should be used with extreme care." I'm exaggerating a bit, but not too much. It's so weird."

I love Brené's down to earth comment on this. I guess most of us tend to take ourselves too seriously, and I think that taking a more grounded approach to telling stories on stage is a wise thing to do. It keeps you in contact with everything that's sincere about you. And that's a place I feel most comfortable in.

Knowing You're Ready To Perform
When do you know exactly that you're ready to perform? We don't have a switch that tells us we're ready. Your safest bet is writing a good piece, rehearsing vigorously, making decisions about visual aids in an early stage, and giving yourself enough time to relax before your performance.

The amount of rehearsing depends on whether you are planning to perform at a TEDx conference or in a corporate setting. Respecting other people's time is always important, but in a corporate setting, there's always slightly more room for improvisation, direct engagement with the audience, answering questions from the audience, and a fair amount of 'shooting from the hip'.

At TEDx, there's almost no room for things like that. This doesn't have to feel like a restriction; it's actually quite the contrary. It's a trigger for you to be more creative in delivering your idea. It gives you more control. Even if monitors remain black. Or if people start laughing over falling stage props. You are in charge of your share of the event. Take charge. It's your moment.

"Presenting is my biggest love, and yet I would rather die twice than go on stage, just before curtain call. But once the show has started, I instantly connect with the audience. It's the only way to deal with it."

—Michèle Sparreboom

INTERVIEW

Michèle Sparreboom:

"By lighting their fire, I light the audience's fire. And my own."

Michèle Sparreboom is a Dutch presenter, talk show host and entrepreneur.

Do you ever feel nervous before you go on stage?
I'm always nervous before going on stage. Always. Presenting is my biggest love, and yet I would rather die twice than go on stage, just before curtain call. But once the show has started, I instantly connect with the audience. It's the only way to deal with it. I just decide to make the room my livingroom, and that the audience is as much part of this gig as I am.

It's very exciting and my love for presenting is big. For me, it's all about curiosity, discovering new things and people. My core feeling while presenting is: it's not about me or about you, it's about us and what we can achieve together.

At times I feel most nervous, I just ask the audience: "Who's afraid to stand on stage? Please show hands!" When I see hands, I say: "So am I! But we're going to make this a super event. Are you with me?" This breaks the ice and it calms my nerves. Behind the scenes, I always have a dry mouth and trembling hands. Fortunately, the love and joy for presenting always win this perpetual intrinsic battle. Love and joy make me want to go that extra mile. And I have trained to manage my heart rate in times of stress. I try to be as nice to myself as I possibly can, because I realize that if you're on stage, you always bring all of yourself with you. And people pick up on tension. You want to share the most accessible version of yourself with them. When I get to that point, as I usually do, my core mission is to lower the threshold for the audience and increase quality as much as humanly possible.

When you're in front of the room and you have to be the taste maker, what do you do to get them all engaged?
Someone once said to me: "I am who I am. Nothing more, nothing less." I consider that to be a golden nugget of wisdom and I use it every time. I aim to facilitate an accessible and pleasant livingroom-like experience, no matter the size of the audience. Nevertheless, I make sure my performance is a professional one, not just a comfortable one. Showing vulnerability and giving your performance a personal touch doesn't say anything about being a professional. But vulnerability and your personal touch do add to an atmosphere that gives the audience a sense of connection, of knowing 'I'm not the only one'. I always use my intuition. I connect visually with people, I look them in the eyes.

How would you define 'owning the stage'?
In my perception, there's no such thing as 'owning a stage'. The only thing you have a fair amount of influence on, is deciding what feeling and what value you can and will contribute to the whole event. What do I want to contribute? That's so important. Far more important than thinking about what you could get out of any particular gig.

Once, I had to perform five days in a row on the largest square in my home town, for a cultural festival. I was the event host. The day before the kick-off event, people were building up the podium and all the stage props. I shuffled past the scaffoldings and thought: "What on earth have I gotten myself into? Why did I agree to do this? Am I good enough?" There is always a moment of doubt. My tip for dealing with this moment is to think in terms of both-and instead of either-or.

In other words: acknowledge and embrace your fear and perform anyway. And prepare yourself properly. Not only in getting all the facts straight before you go on stage, but also on a mental level. Think and decide for yourself with which feeling you wish to leave the stage. And start feeling that emotion right away. Don't ever put off feeling how you wish to feel. This is such a powerful key in presenting, and also in life.

I always prepare for the desired outcome and I start working on making that happen. That way, I'm always halfway there on day one. I care deeply about that.

When does a performance start, and when does it end, for you?
Every performance starts with your preparation. Listening to the people who have invited you to perform. What do they want to get out of it, and how can you make that happen with them and with the audience? That's where I start. My personal preparation is next. My performance isn't over until I have left the stage and when I know that people have had a positive experience.

Who inspires you?
Anyone who knows and lives the art of life. People who know how to love, how to have peace in their lives.

When you truly realize that your performance isn't about you, this deals with the usually unwelcome hurdles of getting one's ego in the way of performing the right way. I always try to find great ideas in people, I learn from them, and I share those ideas by offering these inspiring people my stage. I find inspiring people, collect stories and share them with other people. In my talkshow, I'm always incredibly curious about what I'm going to learn in the next few minutes. By lighting their fire, I light the audience's fire. And my own. You can only make light from light. That's a beautiful concept. My intention for each of my talkshows is that I want to connect people to stories and to each other. It's a privilege. I'm very passionate about this way of working. And every time, it feels like coming home.

Performing at TEDx
shouldn't be a career goal.
It is however something
to take seriously.
Professionals who approach
their TEDx talk as a stepping stone,
take their experience with them
to their next endeavours,
to perform even better.

Just remember that you are
learning until your very last breath.

AFTER TEDx: INVESTING, GROWING, HARVESTING

After TEDxDelft

What has performing at TEDx brought me? What has resonated and what did I discover in the months after?

After the experience, I asked myself whether or not things would have been any different if my talk had been about my work as an online strategist and e-learning specialist, instead about such a personal topic. They probably would have. Performing a talk in sync with my career would have been expected , and I probably would have been proud of it. Nevertheless, I still believe in my decision to share the "idea worth spreading" I wanted to share more than anything. The criteria is still valid.

The first thing I noticed was that the rest of my projects were still there waiting for me. This was something to be very grateful for, since some of my clients had practiced patience. Furthermore, my way of preparing for presentations has slightly changed. Not that I experience every presentation as intensely as the TEDx talk, far from it. But several methods of preparation have stuck with me, and I use them to improve the way I was already presenting, even in corporate settings. My stories are more concise, and I take more time to interact with people after the presentation, more than I already did before.

I still cherish any opportunity for improvisation, because it's just one of the signature elements of my presentations. I wouldn't want to let go of that. My slides also are even simpler than they had been before. Nothing has changed in my visual identity in slide decks; I still use vintage photos. I have a wonderful collection of photos that are over one hundred years old. I find them at thrift stores and in flea markets wherever I travel). I add extra visual layers to them, like blue gradients and typography. The vintage photos provide an extra level of story, metaphor and a visual brand anchor point.

Before the event, you invest a lot of time, effort and sometimes also money. You give and give and give. And if you open your eyes to it, you'll discover that you receive a lot as well afterwards.

Many of my clients have watched the talk, some of them haven't. It has created a new level of depth to the business relationships I already valued so much. In some cases, people were a bit reluctant to watch the talk, because they were afraid that hearing a vulnerable story about my life would move them too much. I cannot change how people feel about me or my talk. I can only act according to my beliefs and moral convictions. So I feel completely at peace with my choice. And it has brought me many wonderful conversations with people I would otherwise probably never have had the pleasure of meeting. I have also learned from people who have read five chapters of my first book for free on one of my websites (WesternOrphans.org). They have shared their own personal stories and written me letters about how they had made financial and foster care arrangements for their children, just in case anything bad ever happened. The talk definitely has opened doors.

What's also refreshingly humbling: where I never used to have pre-presentation jitters, I now (sometimes) do. I don't mind them at all. I embrace them and channel this energy in the right direction.

Thanks to Ric Berretty's awesome tip to use cards with keywords in order to memorize large chunks of copy, I've translated this method also to my business concepts. Often, I carry a pile of cards in my bag, tied up with a rubber band. The cards have become part of just about every conceptual phase of any creative project I work on.

I've also come to value every speaker's route of development, with their own talents, charms, pitfalls and learning curves.

I usually leave my ego at the door and focus even more on providing value (I did that before, but there is still a difference).

What hasn't changed is my speaking style and that I always strive to be original, and to learn, as long as I shall live. I realize that I'll never be done, and I consider that a good thing.

KEY TAKEAWAYS

Recognizing And Creating Opportunities

So you're a speaker, you've learned a lot and accept that this will be an ongoing process. And you're looking for more opportunities to speak and develop your skills. Great! The first thing I think of is: make sure you're already living your ambitions. Try to be on the particular stage you want to be on. Today. I don't mean this in a visualize-your-way-to-bliss way. I mean that you have to be in contact with your primary motivation. I'll give you an example.

The topic of my talk wasn't something I had just thought of a few months before the event. I had already written my book on the topic, had established press coverage about the book publication and had been interviewed by newspapers, glossy magazines and on national and local television. I had published about the topic on websites and blogs since 2007. I had created a body of work even before the TEDx curators decided to invite me. They invited me because I had already proven that I knew a lot about the subject, and still had an "idea worth spreading" that I hadn't shared before. And the timing was right. I was already living my ambition by working on the primary mission. So of course the mission wasn't performing at TEDx. The mission was reaching my goals in raising awareness about orphaned children in Western countries, helping responsible adults facilitate these kids by making a difference in their lives, and empowering kids to build a better life for themselves. TEDx is one of the many stops on a long journey.

You could translate this to your area of expertise and your mission. Ask yourself what your true, primary mission is. Live towards realizing that ambition, and TEDx (or another stage that you're interested in) will be closer than you might think.

If you want to up your game in speaking practically but you're not getting the gigs yet, you might consider doing one of the following things. Apply for roundtable sessions at all kinds of seminars and conferences in your area of expertise. Offer in-company sessions about your topic. Invite other speakers for a gathering around your mutual topic and invite guests. You could also go to a Toastmasters meeting or join other speaking-centered groups. I'm a member of PSA Holland, the Professional Speakers Association.

If you're still stacking up a basic level of experience, you might also offer to speak for your local Rotary club or other business-oriented clubs. And it can't hurt to (get over yourself and) ask for referrals. Share your speaking aspirations on your blog, create a speaker page on your website, join conversations on platforms such as Blab or webinars, embed videos of your performances, update your LinkedIn Professional Headline.

Work on optimizing your elevator pitch, so people in your professional network know what kind of topic you could cover at their events. Mention on Twitter that you're open to speaking engagements. Grow your online network by attracting like-minded people and professionals that correspond with your target group.

Swallow your pride, go out there, let yourself be seen and practice, practice, practice.

Managing Performances
There's always that moment that you should consider hiring an agent to connect you to professional speaking engagements. There are pros and cons in choosing to work with an agent. Any professional who is working with an agent they connect well with, will urge you to find an agent as quickly as possible, especially if you can find an agent who has an immense network and knows-everybody-who-knows-everybody. There are, however, also many professional speakers who like to stay in charge of their own day planner and fee.

So what should you do? To make a long story short: it depends. For starters: if you'll be working with an agent, choose one wisely. I once worked with an agent for just a few weeks.

A renowned agent and has a considerable network. But she was horrible in making deals. She wanted to connect me to an event and offered a much higher fee than I felt comfortable with. My fee at the time was about one thousand five hundred euros for a conference presentation plus a break-out session. It was a job for five hours on location plus a day of preparation. I had been giving presentations for about five years at this point. This wasn't a particularly high fee, but the niche was professionals in public healthcare for a non-profit organization. My agent sent the client a quote for twice that amount and hadn't informed me about this. The client declined the offer (budget reasons: they had to cancel facilities if they had decided to hire me), and called me personally in a very angry tone of voice. I had no idea what had been going on and I promised to take this up with my agent. I called her, and she mentioned that she already lowered my rate to…five hundred euros. I instantly fired her and ordered her to remove my photograph and information from her website. It was without any doubt the most preposterous case of haggling I had ever seen in my life. From that moment on, I decided to handle my own clients. There might come a moment when I decide to work with an agent once more. But in any case, I'll be making an educated decision about that.

The choice whether or not to work with an agent might also have to do with your home country. I've heard that in the U.S., Germany and other countries, it's practically impossible to be taken seriously as a professional speaker if you're answering the phone yourself and/or send quotes to clients for your performances yourself. I've also heard about successful exceptions to that rule, though. In the Netherlands it's still very normal to take on speaking jobs yourself as an entrepreneur, but there are also speaking bureaus. A lot of independent professionals manage their speaking engagements themselves. International speaking gigs are usually managed by an agency, although many professionals prefer to maintain their independence internationally as well.

In the end, you have to decide what suits you best. If you're going about managing your own speaking engagements, make sure you're working on building a professional yet personal brand that suits your speaking topics and your level of expertise.

'Overnight Success'

One of my friends has worked for ten years to build a large audience and client base in her consultancy business, and has put in extra effort to be asked as a speaker at large events. This pays off and her career is developing quickly now, because she has put in the effort for years. Recently she spoke at a large conference in Barcelona, Spain. One of the people in her audience asked her: "How did you become such an overnight success?" This question startled my friend a bit, because she hadn't experienced her ten years of effort as being 'overnight'.

The truth is that your audience doesn't know how long and how hard you have been working on your career. You and I know that it takes a lot of work to get to the point where you are considered a top professional and the go-to person in your area of expertise.

Creating a signature speech, keeping your professional knowledge up to date, growing your client base and building relationships with the press -there's no such thing as being an overnight success in public speaking. It may seem that way to other people. Many professionals have been in business for over ten years, before speaking internationally and reaching new audiences.

Luck

There are always the lucky ones. And then there are the ones who have to struggle for it. But there's a lot of gray in between, fortunately. You always have your unique package of talent, dedication and courage. Luck or no luck, you can always do something to increase your opportunities and success.

The wonderful thing about getting started and relying on your talents, dedication and courage is that your chances of luck increase significantly as you go. You can't force luck, but you can work on creating the ideal circumstances to make things easier.

INTERVIEW

Joleene Moody:

"Trust the journey."

Joleene Moody is a former central New York television reporter and anchor turned freelance writer, blogger, and speaker. After struggling for years in a place that didn't satisfy her true dreams and desires to write for books, stage, and screen, Joleene bravely left the security of her television job to embark on a journey that allowed her to unearth her greatest dreams and desires while profiting generously at the same time. Today she is a powerful mentor to those who want to uncover and discover who and what they are truly meant to be and do. Her motto: "Talents aren't meant to sit idle. They are the key to your absolute abundance. Always." www.joleenemoody.com

Joleene, when did you know the time was right to leave your day job and to pursue a career as an independent public speaker?
I knew when I admitted I was very unhappy and miserable. I dreaded going to work every day. I tried to find the joy in it, but I was ignoring the truth. I think I was probably already building up this unhappiness for three years. At one unfortunate moment, I was reporting on case arraignments about a lady that was murdered. A family member of the deceased woman punched me in the face, out of frustration. It was a confronting moment, and deeply, completely and wholly.

For a while, I kept on going. But a year later, my mother passed away. I got delayed mourning after a while. Eight months later I stopped going to work. This course of events lead me to the point of wanting to change things for the better. My business is going well, and I'm constantly working to improve.

What is your main topic?
My primary theme is that I remind people that they have

"People are always going to tell you what to do.

You have to figure out what it is you want, what you believe and what your guts tell you."

—Joleene Moody

the ability to design their own life. The change is always better than staying where you are. You're gonna feel pain either way: you're going to feel the pain of staying or the pain of change. So if you want to change something for the better, you know you'll have to go through a certain level of discomfort before things improve.

What kind of speaking engagements do you enjoy most?
I like talking to adult learners. That's my favorite. I can share my story and can show them that anything is possible.

Would you consider yourself to be a speaker who relies on rehearsal or improvisation? What is the balance in these two elements in presentation for you?
Rehearsal and improvisation are equally important to me. I prepare for sure. But when I'm in the room, I follow the audience and and dynamic in the room. I pause to answer if there's a question. If this changes the course of the topic, I follow that shift. You need the ability to adjust to changing circumstances.

What is a valuable lesson you've learned as a public speaker? Something you didn't know in your former career as a television personality?
Not everyone will love you. You can't please everybody. The sooner you let go of that, the happier you'll be.

How do you integrate feedback loops in your work as a speaker?
I did a talk last year, I was so criticized. I reported about my history of working at the television network in the city I was speaking. The interesting thing is that one woman took it very personally, and this taught me about people. I didn't apologize.

What was one of the ways you chose to reposition your personal brand from television to keynote speaking?
People in the community knew who I was, and I used that to my advantage. I didn't have a brand. I had my message though, this was: overcoming fear to follow passions. I talked about how scary it was to leave the security of my job. For a little while

it worked, and then I wore the reason out. So then I started to speak regionally and then nationally.

What has proven itself to be an effective marketing strategy for your speaking business?
I would send out a media kit with a book, a brochure, candy and a business card. The message on the box was: "Don't gamble with your next speaker." I called it my "Standout Box Of Confidence."

What do you prefer, marketing via online networks or other ways of marketing?
Frankly: I loathe Facebook ads. I loathe sales funnels. I've used Leadpages, but I didn't have the success that I had anticipated on. I'm just better in converting to sales in a personal way. I have literally earned five figure pay days by simply being in the room and talking to people. I chose to create a circuit, so I made opportunities and got clients from that. I have strong principles: I don't speak unless someone writes me a check.

How do you maintain relationships with your clients, after your performance?
We connect via social media, and I remain very active with them and with some of them, I've become good friends.

A while ago, I was giving business advice and I discovered that I tried to be something I wasn't. I was trying to be a celebrity coach. At the time I had a business coach that was not a nice person, and we stopped working together in 2014. For a year I was healing and realigning. Trying to figure out what to do next. None of it was wrong, because being in the place where I was, I discovered what it was I really wanted. Which was: writing!

The business model that I'm shifting to now, is blogging. I learned how to monetize my blog. And I'm still learning. I do get a lot of traction to my blog. Blogging an interesting way of sharing knowledge and to stay in contact with clients. And it also leads to new speaking engagements.

I feel that my heart is no longer in teaching people this infor-mation. I realized this, but I have to let it go. My blog is for creative entrepreneurs and it's about building it around their talents and their artistic abilities. I believe in that and it feels good.

Do you work with an agent or do you have other sources of assistance?
I have always found my own speaking engagements. It's not true that you need an agent to get gigs. There are speaking professionals who say that you undoubtedly need an agent to be booked. Let me give you an example. Last year in the summer, I organized a Mastermind about finding paid speaking opportunities. People were telling me not to do a Mastermind during the summer, because nobody would sign up for it. Well, the workshop had all twelve places booked, and this also lead to further projects that converted to 45,000 dollars. I learned to be very open-minded, and it pays off.

Whatever you believe, you conceive. People are always going to tell you what to do. You have to figure out what it is you want, what you believe and what your guts tell you.

Because I'm focusing more on my writing now instead of coaching, I'm considering an agent to get me booked for more speaking engagements right now. I'm building traffic to my blog and it's working well. So I want an agent to do the rest of the work for me.

To build and maintain a career as a speaker entrepreneur, it's vital to re-invent yourself from time to time. You evolve as an individual and as a professional. You have also written a book about that. How do you sail through those phases? Do you guide yourself through this, or do you have a coach to help you with this?
I've had coaches, for my business as well as spiritual guidance, but I have decided to follow the guru within. I know what I want. As far as coaching is concerned, I do believe that if you're struggling in money or in growing your business, investing in a coach is the most brilliant thing you can do.

"Trust the journey. If you decide you want to do something different or shift your business, allow that to be okay. Don't listen to the voices that tell you that's wrong, whether it be your own voices or from other people."

—Joleene Moody

Many speakers also start coaching programs. Have you engaged in training clients, either online or in real life?
Yes, I have trained professionals for years, and I'm not going to do that again. I'm a certified coach, but I decided to use that knowledge for the benefit of my writing. I might hire someone to increase my Amazon sales, though. I am selling my books, and every time I do a podcast, I'm selling well. But I think there's more possible.

Who inspires you and influences you in your career as a speaker?
Les Brown was the first speaker I ever heard that made me decide: that is want I want to do with my life. Les is animated and honest.

Trust the journey. If you decide you want to do something different or shift your business, allow that to be okay. Don't listen to the voices that tell you that's wrong, whether it be your own voices or from other people.

The time when speaking
for audiences on stage
in big rooms was the only
way to be widely heard and
seen is behind us.
There are more, other ways
to be heard and seen and
to connect.

Livestreaming video,
real time, all over the world.

CONTINUOUSLY RE-INVENTING YOURSELF IN PUBLIC SPEAKING

Live: Any Time, Any Place

Speaking without the possibility of editing any mistakes out raises the bar. It triggers you to perform even better. And it also makes the whole process somewhat more intimidating. Because you won't get a second chance to make a first impression.

In the last ten years, I've re-invented my style of working in my business. By using digital and social media, I've managed to grow my business since the early days of social media, in a way that suits me. I believe in the power of combining your talents and experience with tools that reinforce those talents and business potential.

Since 2002, I've been posting articles on my blogs. Since 2007, I've been active on Twitter, and I still love it dearly. All social media platforms provide you with means to express yourself and to connect with other people. The combination of taking professional communication to an online level (I've been working as a communication consultant since 2001), expressing myself verbally and connecting with other people on a personal level is something that I embrace fully.

Video Livestreaming Back In The Day
In 2009, I started experimenting with video livestreaming with my iPhone, with apps such as Qik and Ustream. Mobile data bundles weren't common back then, so this often resulted in high phone bills.

Another reason that video livestreaming wasn't used as much as it is today was that it wasn't possible to communicate with other people in your video livestream. You could check Twitter for replies to your account, but you had to leave your mobile video app in order to do so. The lack of real-time communication while broadcasting created this hurdle that couldn't be fixed at that moment in digital development. But when mobile video livestreaming platforms Meerkat and Periscope launched consecutively in January and March 2015, I started video livestreaming again, with great enthusiasm. Since it became possible to communicate with other people in real time during the video broadcast, this was a welcome addition to my online communication arsenal. Blab, Snapchat and Facebook Live prove themselves to be useful for branding and business.

The time when speaking for audiences on stage in big rooms was the only way to be heard and seen is behind us. There are other ways to be heard and seen besides real life.

Livestreaming in real life presentations

Since the moment that real life presentations began being livestreamed online, it became possible to learn from experts without leaving your office or living room. Most TEDx conference are being livestreamed. This is a valuable, because tickets to these events tend to sell out quickly. Via livestreaming, anyone has the opportunity to witness what is happening on stage, in real time.

A few years ago, event organizers were not particularly keen on livestreaming integral events, because they feared ticket sales would go down dramatically. This fear proved itself to be unfounded, since (especially) TEDx events are still extremely valuable to attend in real life. You get a chance to meet amazing people who are all very open to discovering new ideas. TEDx tickets still sell out quickly. We can conclude that sharing content in real time online has even contributed a great deal to the TEDx experience. If you look at the number of times that many TEDx talks have been viewed on YouTube, you understand why.

The same benefit is applicable for other events as well. Event organizers can choose to make part of their program available on an online video channel. Another excellent example of an event that decided to share their content is The Next Web (always sold out early). It's a great way to discover novelties in technology, online communications and all things social and mobile.

Livestreaming online conferences

Since the online birth of Blab.im, it became possible to organize online conferences, without hiring a professional video and sound crew, renting a location and other overhead costs. On January 29th 2016, I organized the first international online conference from the Netherlands: Beyond Envy Conference 2016. We had a great lineup of thirteen international speakers, who were all willing to share valuable insights about their professional expertise. The conference provided seven hours of ongoing in-depth discussion and value.

It may have been cost effective, but it was an enormous amount of work in terms of organizing the event, inviting speakers, making sure the technology would work brilliantly, instructing the Production Team and facilitating everyone with every resource they needed in order to give a great performance. I worked for fourteen days non-stop to get it all ready. Long days, short nights.

I have been blessed to be able to work with an exceptionally capable and innovative Production Team lead by Lori Webb. Lori is from the United States originally, lives in Kopenhagen, Denmark and she works internationally. Lori is also the (pending) Guinness Book of Records record holder for organizing the longest livestream event ever; she hosted The Big Blab during a seven day period, twenty-four hours a day. The hashtag was #the168. It was amazing. And of course I trusted Lori completely with my own conference that would be seven hours in one go. She and her team (Jonathan Tripp, Frank Clark, Zef Zan) and my production assistants (Alex Keizer and Caroline Verhees) have done an excellent job. My speakers and I are very grateful. And this event most definitely opened up a lot of new doors for me professionally.

After the event, I was invited to even more online conferences, organized by other innovative professionals, and I decided to host my own OnlineComm Live! shows. This works brilliantly for me. And another advantage is that I still get booked to speak at events, in my own country and abroad.

Educational purposes
Online livestream sessions are very useful for educational purposes. In my online courses, I use video livestreaming for call-ins with my students, and I provide them with updates about online novelties that they can use in their assignments and own professional practice. We use platforms such as Appear.in, Zoom.us, Skype and Room.co. And if we want to have a public discussion, we engage in conversations via Blab. And on my own secure e-learning platform OnlineComm Academy, I have created about six hundred training videos about online strategy, social media marketing, communications and online tools.

Social Radio conversations
Since the moment social radio tool Anchor was launched, it became possible to engage in conversations with other people via short sound fragments, recorded with a smartphone. It's a wonderful way to have quality conversations about an array of topics, such as online conferences, online livestreamed conferences with Blab, Periscope livestreaming, Interactive Radio and Videoconferencing.

Erasing geographical borders, expanding reach
When I organized the first online conference via livestreaming application Blab.im ever (from the Netherlands), my network expanded enormously in a matter of weeks. Video livestreaming is a powerful and essential part of my communication eco system.

Repurposing your talks
Creating durable value is easy, once you have a great topic and content. If you're broadcasting via livestreaming video, you can easily make recordings. You can use video files and make them available for your network. For instance, you can make a collection of your livestream talkshows and make this series available in an online course, or as a free gift for people who sign up for your newsletter. And my Beyond Envy Conference 2016 is still available online for everyone to enjoy at www.beyondenvyconference.com.

INTERVIEW

Jet Sol:

"Take your audience on an adventure in your story.

Jet Sol is a Dutch television personality and television program creator.

Jet, you have been on television for many years now. Although you aren't a public speaker in the classical definition of the word, you do have much experience in speaking to crowds and sharing experiences in documentaries and other television programs. I value insights from many disciplines, and I believe public speakers could benefit a great deal from your insights. Would you share some of your experiences that might help public speakers?
"The challenge is to let yourself and your audience go on an adventure in your story. Take them with you. Have the courage to show yourself in different situations, without being easy on yourself. Don't over-polish. Not your story, nor your position in your story. Don't aim to be the one who looks the best in your stories. Sometimes you have to sacrifice your own polished image for the sake of letting the story thrive."

How do you feel about scripted presentations? Do you use them on television?
"At the moment, I'm working on a television series that I enjoy very, very much. We don't use a teleprompter. We just prepare very well for the kick-off of every episode. After that, we have no idea what will happen. That is part of the fun and of the program value. It is most definitely authentic, every moment you see in every show. The concept is that in each episode, I walk a straight line through a part of my county. Literally. This means that I have to climb over fences, ring doorbells to go through people's homes, sometimes I have to wade through muddy, watery ditches or climb over ladders in order to cross a small river. The core message of the program is that we meet a lot of people, who sometimes help

us a great deal. And sometimes, these people share heartfelt stories. This is how we want to show our county to our viewers. They recognize themselves, their neighbours and people from other cities than their own.

Frankly, we never know what we're up against every week. This means that we have to improvise a lot. We have a small television team: the camera woman, the sound man and myself. The three of us are a solid team. And I never ask for vanity editing of the episodes. If I climb over a fence in a not so flattering way, I won't be the one complaining with the editor. We show things as they happen. It's informative, quirky and entertaining."

Despite the fact that the concept flirts with reality-tv, it's always tasteful.
"Because it isn't about us. It's about the people we meet. We show our conversations and let the viewers be part of other people's lives for just a moment. Sometimes, we go back to people we met earlier in a television season. The stories that touched our hearts are so inviting, that we ask if we can visit these people once more, to see how they are doing six months later. Because we care."

The show is about the people you meet. But it's also about the viewers.
"Yes. They can connect with people in the show by feeling joy, empathy, interest or any other emotion, from a safe distance. And because we do not spare me in the show, people tend to appreciate the stories even more. So in a way, I'm the constant in the show, because I cross our county. I am the presenter. But I choose to play with this role. Because everyone can relate to the everyday adventures I encounter in the show."

I think it's lovely that you choose to show your own personality in your show, professional and frivolous. You can't fake that.
"You can't fake that, and you shouldn't."

Where can message and improvisation collide?
"Let your message be your compass, but stay on course.

And if you have the opportunity to improvise in a way that your audience will resonate even more to your message, do it. Seize opportunity when it presents itself. If you are not bound to a script, teleprompter or something like that, then try to have faith in the good outcome. Prepare as well as you can, and create the circumstances in which unexpected beautiful things can emerge. When you see these gems, grab them. That's the adventure in it. And what fun is your job if you're not making the most of the experience?"

In order to be able to speak well, you need to develop and nourish your ability to listen intentionally and with all your presence and attention for other people.

With your eyes, ears and heart wide open, with all pure intention to connect with them. With empathy. Then, and only then, can you learn to speak, perform and resonate. Make the stage your sacred ground for your unique "idea worth spreading."

DISCOVER MORE

The day before the manuscript of the book you're holding right now had to go through the editing process, I was scanning the chapters, checking if I had included all of the necessary stories and key takeaways. I was writing in the cafeteria of the Aula Congress Centre of Delft, University of Technology, which was also the location of the TEDxDelft conference the year before. I was hoping that returning to this location would provide me with a bit of luck on Deadline Day.

That day, February 24th, would also have been my biological father's ninety-first birthday. That whole day evolved around the theme 'fathers'. About my own father, about my foster dad, and also about other people's fathers. Next to my table in the university cafeteria where I sat writing, were three people discussing the difficult situation one of them was dealing with. I glanced at the woman who was sharing her struggle. She looked very much like my own sister, who emigrated from the Netherlands to the United States in 2014.

The woman sitting next to me in the cafeteria had lost her husband a year before. She and her two children were trying to make things work as best as they could, but were struggling along the way. Both children were coping in different ways. It made me think of how my sister and I had been struggling with our losses, with equal pain, but in different ways and with different personalities. The echo of our personal stories and the story of the lady sitting next to me touched my heart. I took the opportunity to reach out to her, and to tell her that someone recognizes her and her children's struggle. It was a positive encounter.

It fills my heart with so much love and gratitude that sharing my experiences and tips for people around orphaned children can make a difference in other people's lives. But being truly heard and seen is something I can provide for other people. It is my way of trying to be the empathic adult I needed so much when my parents had just passed away.

In order to be able to speak well, you need to develop and nourish your ability to listen intentionally and with all your presence and attention for other people. With your eyes, ears and heart wide open, with all pure intention to connect with them. With empathy. Then, and only then, can you learn to speak, perform and resonate. Make the stage your sacred ground for your unique "idea worth spreading."

LEARNING MORE

If you want to up your performance as a speaker, you can of course experiment all you want with the tips that you have found in this book. Some of the tips for TEDx talks can also be very useful if you're preparing for a corporate presentation or for other speaking engagements. For a broad spectrum of insights on public speaking, I recommend 'The Art of Public Speaking' by Dale Carnegie (1888-1955). It's a classic.

If you're looking for a speaker coach who can assist you individually and in real life sessions, there are several routes you could take. You could do a quick search on Google for 'speaker coach' in your area. You can of course also find out who the speaker coaches for TEDx conferences are in your area and contact them. Many TEDx speaker coaches are also taking clients. If you're looking for a speaker coach with another goal in mind than a TEDx performance, you still might benefit from these professionals. If you search on Google for 'corporate speaking coach' in your area, you'll find more 'all-around' speaker coaches.

You might consider contacting the Global Speakers Federation (globalspeakersfederation.net), the Professional Speakers Asso-ciation in your country (for instance PSAHolland.org), the National Speakers Association in the United States (nsaspeaker.org), and many other organizations that are a meeting point for professional speakers all over the world. Some (not all) of the members are also speaker coaches. I am a member of PSA Holland and the Global

Speakers Federation. Sometimes I help people to improve their performance, but this is not my core business. My company OnlineComm Academy teaches people to optimize their online communication strategy and teaches them how to use digital platforms and social media effectively. My company is also the initiator of the social sustainability projects WesternOrphans.org and its Dutch equivalent (WeesWijzer.nu).

Jojanneke's Speaking Topics
You can book me as a speaker for your event about the following topics.

- How to develop your online communication and social media strategy

- The difference between corporate presentations and TEDx talks and how to improve your performance:
www.liveyourtalks.com

- How to leverage video livestreaming for your business:
www.livestreamforbusiness.com

- E-learning innovation and how to optimize your online courses:
www.social-elearning.com

- How to notice, facilitate and empower orphaned children in the Western world
www.WesternOrphans.org

Bookings
Bookings via www.jojannekevandenbosch.com.

Social media
Connect with me via Twitter: @jojanneke
LinkedIn: www.linkedin.com/in/jojannekevandenbosch
Blab.im/jojanneke

"That process of becoming who you really are, through performing, through releasing, and you connecting to the audience. With that process, something greater can happen. It's what we want in life: for our experiences to open up. Go deep. Dig deeper."

—Hugh Jackman, *Inside the Actor's Studio*

THANK YOU

"Family isn't always blood. It's the people in your life who want you in theirs; the ones who accept you for who you are. The ones who would do anything to see you smile and who love you, no matter what."

Thank you, Mama and Papa, IP, Coen van der Lugt, Marianne van der Lugt-van 't Hof, Eveline van der Lugt-Buiteman, Alex Keizer.

TEDxDelft curators: Rob Speekenbrink, Jeroen van Erp, Caryn 't Hart de Wijckerslooth.

Performance coach and director: Ric Berretty.
TEDxDelft speaker coaches: Jet van Paassen, Toine Andernach.

Friends who helped me prepare for the talk: Lotje Paauwe, Wieneke Gunneweg, Martèn de Prez, Daan Westerink, Mariken Spuij, Hennie Tibben, Dick & Mary Zevenhuizen.

The experts who have generously shared their insights:
Buffi Duberman, Lianne Ebbinkhuijsen, Else Kramer, Joleene Moody, Edo van Santen, Henkjan Smits, Jet Sol, Amy van Son, Soness Stevens, Michèle Sparreboom.

My dear editor: Leah Krevit, Texas, USA.

Delft University of Technology janitors of Aula Conference Center, Cafe Vlaanderen.

Thank you for inspiring me and for existing:
Guy Kawasaki and Shawn Welch (for your book A.P.E.).
Todd Herman, for providing me with the fantastic 'The 90 Day Year' mindset. Gabriel Byrne, for inspiring me to finish writing the first book as quickly as humanly possible, which lead to improved policy for orphaned children in the Netherlands.

You, for taking the time to read this book.

So, you've read this book. What is the first thing you will do to improve your presentation skills?

- ☐ watch more TED and TEDx talks
- ☐ bingewatch my favorite series on demand
- ☐ practice and record my pitch video for a local TEDx conference
- ☐ take a course in mime
- ☐ stop asking me questions, will you
- ☐ join a local speaking association
- ☐ practice speaking in another language
- ☐ experiment with video livestreaming
- ☐ write my thank you notes for TEDx, just in case
- ☐ *knock knock*

www.ingramcontent.com/pod-product-compliance
Lightning Source LLC
Chambersburg PA
CBHW061639040426
42446CB00010B/1494